WRITING POETRY

The Essential Guide

Need
– 2 –
Know

First published in Great Britain in 2001 by
Writers' Bookshop.
Writers' Bookshop is an imprint of Forward Press Ltd.

Second Edition published in Great Britain in 2010 by
Need2Know
Remus House
Coltsfoot Drive
Peterborough
PE2 9JX
Telephone 01733 898103
Fax 01733 313524
www.need2knowbooks.co.uk

Need2Know is an imprint of Forward Press Ltd.
www.forwardpress.co.uk
All Rights Reserved
© Kenneth Steven 2010
SB ISBN 978-1-86144-112-6
Cover photographs: Dreamstime

Contents

Introduction

Being asked to write about the composition of poetry and how to do the job better might be considered something like being invited to accept the throne in the Middle Ages. A very dangerous job indeed.

It's hard enough being a poet and understanding what the ingredients are that makes a poem good without then having to turn round and explain that process to others.

Let me say from the outset that I don't believe that I or anyone else can hope to create a poet from nothing. The Greeks knew what they were talking about when they imagined the Muses, the creatures from the realm beyond who brought into our world gifts of poetic inspiration for those with pen in hand who strove for majestic language and divine ideas. They were right – the transmission of poetic inspiration really is inexplicable; the author may well look at a poem the day after composing it and wonder at the imagery, the use of verbs, and so on. The poet was so caught up by the power of inspiration that the conscious mind did not interfere with the putting down of the words. And it's somewhere in there that the Muse appears – that's the magic.

If the writing of poetry could be taught like algebra or history – and heaven forbid – then the process would be tied down to earth and made of clay. The fact is that it is of the angels, and though bits of the skirts of it sometimes dance close enough to us that we can catch them for a moment, for the most part they remain beyond our reach for us to marvel at and dream for, like children watching a basket balloon in the sky.

Some people reading this book may feel tired by their own efforts; they may believe that anything they write is just shadow-play in comparison with the compositions of the true greats. They may argue there is no mortal point writing another poem about a rainbow or a sunset or a robin in winter because all of these subjects have been done to death, written about and immortalised since the day the first poet decided to put pen to papyrus.

'If the writing of poetry could be taught like algebra or history – and heaven forbid – the process would be tied down to earth and made of clay.'

But the exciting thing is that though it's absolutely true that 10,564 poems may have been composed about sunsets before, no one has seen the sunset you see, no one has seen it through your eyes. So the particular words you find for your poem – if you can allow the magic of the Muse to give you wings – will make your composition unique. It will move people, it will make them see a sunset in a new and special way.

So this book is for those who already love poetry, those who are readers of the genre and those who have been caught up in its spell. It is for those who have written poetry and who are perhaps dispirited because what they have written does not correspond with the original idea of the poem they had in their mind.

It is for those who are frustrated by half-finished poems buried in drawers, by rhyming verse that loses the point, by writing they love but which everyone else criticises or doesn't relate to. And it is for those who are quite satisfied with what they have written but want challenge and new direction, poetic gymnastics to enable them to chart different territory.

What I can't impart is the initial inspiration to write poetry; what I hope I can give is advice on composing richer, more dynamic poetry and on capturing those priceless ideas more exactly, more satisfyingly.

I am a professional writer and, for better or worse, the majority of the work I produce as a poet is intended for publication. (That doesn't prevent a very great deal of it ending up lighting my winter fire because it hasn't gone the way I imagined or else has broken down midway through.) However, I want to make it clear that this book is for people who enjoy reading and writing poetry; it is not for some kind of social elite who have published a certain number of poems or indeed who may have that as their primary goal in life.

In this guide, we will cover the following topics:

- Rhythm and rhyme, verbs, sounds in poetry, alliteration and assonance.
- Writing conditions: the nature of poetry, time, creative techniques and ideas.
- Editing: a time and a place, learning the process.
- Structuring a poem.
- Writing exercises and diary poems.
- Writing to heal.

- Poetry for children – language, verse writing to publish, collections.

The most exciting thing I discover as I travel all over Britain visiting writers' groups and undertaking workshops is that individuals from every walk of life imaginable are writing poetry: cleaners, firemen, doctors, foresters, gardeners, and so on. Each one of them is bringing their own particular experience of the world to life when they start to write; their insights, their memories, their experiences – both good and bad, their visions of the future.

You do not need a degree in English literature to write poetry (in fact some people would argue that a degree would hinder you from the start!), nor do you need to possess the right accent. You need imagination, sensitivity, inspiration and dedication. The vast majority of those individuals I have the privilege of meeting are not writing because they have pretensions to bring out a collection with Faber and Faber or any other grand publisher, they are writing purely and simply because they love poetry. They write because not doing it would be impossible.

Chapter One

What is Poetry?

Defining poetry is not an easy task, and it's one that has become increasingly difficult as poetry and prose as genres of literature have moved closer together.

Until the beginning of the 20th century, rhyme was the order of the day; in the wake of the First World War, all that had been taken for granted as far as the writing of poetry in Europe was thrown into question. People were asking themselves what the whole purpose of life was; they began to question whether there could be a god at all who allowed such appalling suffering. They asked most of all what the future of such a world would be, where machines killed ever-increasing numbers of human beings and where civilians would never be safe again from the attacks of their enemies. All of these questions threw artists from every discipline into disarray and made them begin to question the set forms that had been so accepted in years before.

I don't want to go into too much detail here as far as rhyme itself is concerned because a whole section of this book is going to be devoted to the topic. But someone at a writing workshop recently challenged me by declaring that what was described as poetry in today's world just wasn't because it didn't rhyme. He described the best of it as good poetic prose, but no more than that. It set me thinking and I concluded that for him then the main criterion of a poem was that it rhymed. There our paths part company; poetry for me is about many more things than rhyme or the lack of it.

Poetry is to prose what dancing is to walking

This was the definition someone once gave of poetry – and I think it's powerful. The short lyric poem is generally attempting to capture a single moment, an emotion, a place in just a few 'heightened' words. There is no room for padding, for all the extra baggage that might be expected in the novel or even in the short story. The thing is pruned down and down until it is just a core, a heart. The words themselves create the emotion – and this is the crucial thing to my mind – it is the very sound content and pattern of the individual words and their arrangement which makes poetry.

In that sense, the poem has something in common with the song. The very musicality of each word and its position in association with the others is important.

I think of the first words of the first line of Robert Frost's oft-quoted *Stopping by Woods on a Snowy Evening*:

Whose woods these are I think I know

'It is the magic of the human voice – and preferably the poet's own – that awakens the patterns of carefully woven syllables and vowels.'

No one I've ever met would begin a piece of prose, either written or spoken, in such an odd manner! But it isn't just change for the sake of change; Frost is acutely aware of the power of sound in the poem and from the very first syllable he makes that clear. The whole poem is about the deep snows in a forest in mid-winter; Frost creates a perfect sense of the depth of snow just by the sounds of his words!

I often ask children in primary schools exactly what sort of wintry scene they picture us observing; they are never in any doubt about the answer. They are absolutely convinced (although the poem never actually spells it out) that the snow is deep and muffling and that the falling flakes are real cats' paws of snow! Frost's sounds are woolly and gentle and soft and simple; almost every word in the poem is a single syllable so that each becomes like a new heavy flake of snow itself.

So sound is central to the working of the poem. Indeed I feel that it is so important that poems really should be read aloud to bring them fully to life (of course that is precisely why there are so many poetry readings all over the country and across the world!). It is the magic of the human voice – and preferably the poet's own – that awakens the patterns of carefully woven syllables and vowels.

Being conscious of the kind of picture and mood you want to create in the poem from the outset is of prime importance, though it doesn't need to be and really shouldn't be a deliberate and imprisoning process. For most people it is entirely natural because we are aware of what our mother tongue gives us in terms of hard and soft, threatening and gentle, mysterious and frightening words. But it's valuable to look at our writing more closely to see how sound is at work and to see how the effects of sound can best be strengthened and increased. Later I'll be looking at one particular poem in its entirety to break down the sound effects and their locations.

Rhythm

Again there's a link here with the song, with musicality. Rhythm accentuates the mood of the poem, its whole meaning and purpose and movement.

Consider:

> The way the silver light moves soft and slow and clear...

It's obvious what the intention is and what mood is being created even from observing these first few words; indeed I almost believe it would be possible to write an essay about the poem as a whole just on the basis of that first line! The rhythm constitutes gentleness and reflection, a pastoral scene that describes a moment, a frozen moment in time. All the same the poet may choose to build such a rhythm to lull the reader into a false sense of security; the moment might well be broken by a sudden intrusion, either human or otherwise. In that instance the rhythm would change in a bang, and the jarring distortion would create a new pace altogether, perhaps discordant and threatening, or one that is much faster so that the reader immediately speeds up their own absorption of the words (especially useful when building up a sense of tension.)

'Rhythm accentuates the mood of the poem, its whole meaning and purpose and movement.'

Examples

- Read the work of the First World War poets – Wilfred Owen and Siegfried Sassoon in particular – and you will become aware of how well-versed (excuse the obvious pun) they were in the use of rhythm. They both came from a tradition which took rhythm and rhyme for granted; both of them were very familiar with the work of Romantic poets like Keats and Shelley in particular (see book list for suggestions, or search online for examples of their work).

- In Owen's poems especially, the rhythm and rhymes we expect are often deliberately broken. We read the lines wanting the right number of syllables and the rhyming words which we expect and hope for, and we are often disappointed. He breaks them just slightly, but enough to communicate cleverly and powerfully the feeling of nervousness and ill-ease which was being felt by all the soldiers along the Front. By using these broken rhythms and non-fulfilled half-rhymes, he makes us feel just the same restlessness and anxiety.

Rhythm is being lost altogether in much of the poetry being published today. Perhaps that's because poets want to communicate the purposelessness of much of our society's existence and the search there is amid materialism and secular living for deeper meaning and fulfilment.

But understanding how rhythm works and how it may be manipulated are important skills indeed. It's a bit like learning to skate.

> 'The little dancers of poetry are verbs. Verbs create movement, vitality, sparkle; if chosen well, they can do the work of a whole string of adjectives and/or adverbs, but without adding superfluous weight.'

Adjectives and verbs

Adjectives: describing work

Most people starting to write poetry pepper their work with adjectives. We're all taught this in school – and quite rightly – that it's the adjectives that do the describing work, they are the cart horses of descriptive writing. So it's little wonder that when folk come to poetry they throw adjectives to left and to right in the confident belief that it's going to make their poetry sing.

The problem is that adjectives are too powerful; I describe them as having the effect of acting like lugubrious tortoises – they slow lines down. Even in prose, adjectives need to be handled with caution; of course in the right place they can be used by the shovelful and effectively so, it's just important to learn when they're going to be a burden and when they'll prove a blessing. So it's important to ask yourself whether your adjectives are justified or not; if they're doing what they're supposed to do or just simply getting in the way.

Verbs: the dancers of poetry

Verbs create movement, vitality, sparkle; if chosen well they can do the work of a whole string of adjectives and/or adverbs, but without adding superfluous weight. English is a language equipped with magnificent verbs; many of them are full of the sound of the thing they are acting out (onomatopoeic) and so become perfect for use in poetry.

A reasonable poem can be elevated in status to a really great poem by listening to and polishing the verbs. Most of the time, the poet starting out will write when describing the rain that it is 'trickling down the walls'. But why write trickling instead of trying to find a verb that really sings with the music of rain. In a country with at least 50 different types of rain, there should be at least 50 verbs to describe the varying degrees! Verbs that are made out of nouns, verbs that have as their root the names of musical instruments, verbs that are whispers and verbs that are positively crashing with the heavy grapes of thunder rain. Trickling is the verb that all the other poets used; why don't you find something different, something that describes your rain?

I try to make it a rule that I never leave a new poem before reading the verbs aloud to ensure they are offering something new and vibrant and challenging. Because some of the verbs I find are just too different and strange, a good percentage of my poems will fail, but it's better to fail having been daring than to end up with a poem that people politely describe as 'nice'. Your job is to move people, to inspire people – to make them think of things and see things in new ways.

Go and read the early poems of Seamus Heaney and Ted Hughes in particular. Their whole character as people and as poets is conveyed through their verbs: their fierce love and knowledge of the countryside, their desperate desire to create great canvases that capture their childhood haunts, and their history, wild creatures and unique characters. In one poem, Heaney even talks (as if to the Muse) about his wish to be transformed into 'pure verb', and I think I know exactly what he's getting at. He realises that verbs are the heavyweight champions of great poems and he is searching and sifting them like a gold panner on the hunt for nuggets in a river. He wants all of them and he wants the best!

Playing games with words

I think we often forget just how old our language is and what its roots are. I often ask primary children to imagine they're not sitting at all in a modern, faceless classroom with traffic battering up and down the main road beyond the school walls. I ask them to imagine instead that they are living in Stone Age times, huddled together in a great cave at night. Their world is totally and utterly dark – and dangerous. Why would language and communication be useful to them?

Well, the obvious answer is for painting pictures. We needed to provide each other with pictures in words so that we would be able to communicate warnings of wild animals, images of places either threatening or safe, and the shape of the landscape round about.

Just think of the word flint. Try to imagine you had never held a piece or brought sparks from it with another stone, that you did not know what it was at all in fact. The very word is made up of a main, hard sound that has a sharpness to it.

Compare flint with clay, a word that immediately sounds softer because of the consonants and the ending that drifts away rather than banging shut as the first did. There is almost an understanding in the word clay that this is something malleable. And how old do you suppose the word snow is? Say it aloud and hear the flow of it – fairly ridiculous to imagine without knowing its meaning that it might be a hard or sharp substance. Little likelihood of foreigners believing that it might be an offensive weapon! Rather it melts in the mouth, has a soft gentleness to it.

If you've studied another language then compare nouns and their sounds both in that language and in English (particularly relevant in the case of Indo-European languages). The patterns are likely to be just the same; our ancestors everywhere were all doing the same thing – creating pictures of the world about them using sounds that would best capture their colour, shape, texture and feel.

Sounds in poetry

That's the springboard into poetry. Having thought about groups of words and the sounds that characterise them, take a subject and group around it the various sounds that you intuitively feel should be associated with it. A 'cluster' poem would be nothing more than an onomatopoeic description of the subject in as concise a way as possible. Let's say we choose a waterfall; it's not the ideas that might surround it that matter to begin with, it's nothing more than the very core nature of the waterfall – what it sounds like, feels like, looks like:

> *Gush of silver flutes*
> *Riding the blue sky*
> *A tail of tangled threads*
> *Silver and blue*
> *To crash down loud on stone*
> *Swirl into wild pools.*

The idea is that almost in the same way as a riddle, a reader should be able to absorb the words and guess the title without having to know it or read it. Notice that the first four lines of my fragment are completely different sound-wise to the final two. That was not planned deliberately at all, but it works because there has been a subtle change in the nature of the description within the poem. The water, having leapt over the high gullet of rocks and gone into freefall, then splashes over stones at the bottom and runs out into new pools. The sounds describe that change; in the opening section they are high, light and thin sounds, but when the fall is ended, the language becomes darker and heavier, stronger and more aggressive.

Practise this for yourself by using the following steps:

- Look and listen. Imagine you're a child again, or someone landing here from the planet Eclipton.

- See it all for the first time.

- Let impressions really touch you, use all of your senses to absorb either an urban or a country world.

Practise these steps because your poetry will benefit as a result – without a doubt. That doesn't mean that you should become so conscious of sound in your poems that it interrupts entirely the flow of your imaginative thought. I mean rather that when thinking about the poem you are going to write, you are aware of the kind of words you are searching for, and that when revising you are conscious of the 'world' of the poem you were trying to create. You know the atmosphere you intended to capture and you can adjudge whether or not the sounds you built together assist in gathering a 'globe' of linked patterns.

In doing so, you can weed out words that just don't fit, whose sounds mitigate against your intentions in the poem. It won't be relevant for all of the work you create – it really depends to a large extent on what type of poetry you are most drawn to – but in environmental writing in particular and in work that deals with a single charged moment in time, chisel and polish your sounds until they shine.

'...in environmental writing in particular and in work that deals with a single charged moment in time, chisel and polish your sounds until they shine.'

Alliteration and assonance

Once we realise just how powerful sounds are and how very much they contribute to the 'world' of the poem, we can begin to learn how best to harness that power through using different tools.

One way of achieving this is by repeating both consonant and vowel sounds; the effect of this is to reinforce the picture that the sound pattern creates – either for a reflective and tranquil description or else a violent and tempestuous one, and so on:

> The trees thrashed their brassy branches
> Against the yellow anger of the skies.

The poet is attempting to capture as much drama and danger in the scene as possible; the hard sounds of the shaking trees are more powerfully reinforced by the alliterative 'br' of the adjacent adjective and noun. This is a very aggressive example of the use of alliteration, but the effect can be demonstrated quite differently:

> Slow from the slumber of the river stones
> The snake slid forth in silver coils.

I have exaggerated this deliberately so as to make the effect as obvious as possible, but it's important when discovering and using alliteration for the first time that one doesn't do it to death. The poor poet Gerard Manley Hopkins, a Jesuit poet from the Victorian era, became utterly obsessed with alliteration to such an extent that his later poems are all but tongue twisters. The moral of the story is to be sparing and careful when employing alliteration – don't let it jump into every verse as its effect will be crass and overdone.

Back to the snake poem. I deliberately started the first line with the verb slow; the line does not read terribly easily or naturally (as prose might) and this helps to keep the pace calm and unhurried. Thus the effect of the snake's movement is further captured. But what is even more important in the two lines is the continued repetition of the 's' sound. It creates softness, suggests calm and regular movement (going back to the thought of where language stems from, just think of all the nouns and adjectives designed to calm that are full to the brim with 's' sounds!).

There is something else; we associate snakes with the hissing they make (rather in stereotypical terms, and we teach it from the onset of childhood), and that hissing is at least hinted at in the use of the 's' sounds. I wanted to suggest a tongue flicking out as the snake passed over the stones – the possibility of a slight hissing – soft and controlled but also menacing. The alliteration and the slow pace of the lines may well be lulling the reader into a false sense of security prior to a rather nasty and bad bite!

Someone once described assonance as bad rhyme. That was very harsh and unhelpful too, I think. Just in the same way in which alliteration can help to reinforce consonant sound patterns to create more vivid pictures, so vowels can do this in assonance:

> Against the long dark shadows thronged
> The orange lanterns flickered, ominous, sick...

I hope that even without the adjective 'ominous' in the second line of this that the background to the whole poem might be identifiable from the word go. I have used several devices here to build the scene; first of all there is the use of longer lines to slow the reader down and to build tension. As part of this, there is also polysyllabic and complex vocabulary. The sounds in general are deliberately sombre and bleak; I wanted to suggest darkness and a thoroughly dangerous place.

'Whether you're using assonance or alliteration, the game is the same – be subtle and sparing, take a delicate brush rather than a sledgehammer.'

But finally, and most importantly, there's the assonance. Here I've used the drawn-out 'o' sound to make the picture more melancholic still. I do so as subtly as possible; the pattern is random and only occasional so that the reader will not be fully aware of it, or at least not over-aware of it (there is little point putting three or more same vowel-linked words side by side because the effect will be overkill). In this kind of description, it would be the equivalent in cinematic terms of draping the walls with decaying bats and the skulls of rodents!

It's always better to underwrite than to overwrite. Aim rather for something like a drumbeat that sounds once, is silent, then echoes again, disappears, then comes back at last for a third and final time.

Whether you're using assonance or alliteration, the game is the same – be subtle and sparing, take a delicate brush rather than a sledgehammer.

Summing Up

- Sound is central to the working of a poem – so be creative.

- Poems should be read aloud to bring them fully to life.

- Be careful with how many adjectives you use.

- Verbs create movement in a poem – if chosen well they can do the work of a whole string of adjectives and/or adverbs.

- Alliteration and assonance are tools which can be used to create powerful sounds in poetry.

- Read the work of the poets listed in this chapter for inspiration.

Chapter Two
Writing Conditions

The nature of poetry

When I hear from individuals or from writers' groups that creative inspiration comes easily to them and is never a struggle, I tend to take it with more than a pinch of salt. It really is true for all genres: writing is a process that demands great energy and concentration, and very rarely (if ever) can it be turned on and off like the proverbial tap.

But of course there is a difference between poetry and the other genres that I already outlined at the start of this book; poetry is all about the working of the subconscious and the releasing of the fire that is sparked by that. I don't believe it's arrogant to suggest that writing poetry is a deeper process, a more concentrated and demanding one.

People have occasionally commented to me that I looked thoroughly drained in the wake of completing a poem; I can only remember feeling a sense of exhilaration that I had got down on paper the words that were haunting my head. But certainly it would have been almost impossible to think of beginning work that was intellectually challenging just after finishing the poem – tired I certainly was!

It isn't just about the subconscious, it's to do with emotions too. Most of us who are moved to write poetry – whether several times a week or a handful of times in the course of a lifetime – do so because we have been moved by some elemental emotion. By that I mean that we are grieving over something or someone, celebrating or suffering love, or attempting to put into words feelings of immense joy. Just as emotions in everyday life cause tears and pain

'One sure way to avoid becoming stale is to read; when you're tired of reading the work of one author then read that of another.'

and immense elation, so the emotions we capture in the words of poems tear out of us reflections of those same emotions. That hurts and costs – just as life does.

The more hurry

All this means that you shouldn't try to wring four or five poems out of yourself in a single day – there are no hospitals catering for patients suffering from poetic exhaustion!

I think at the beginning we all may be liable to do this – it's like the novelty of finding we can skate for the first time. Once we start we just don't want to stop. But because of the deep emotional level to which we should be reaching to convey those thoughts and feelings in our poetry, we should neither expect nor want to pour out reams of this every day. Being a sensitive person at the best of times is a tiring business – there is a danger of taking all the cares of the world upon one's shoulders.

And yet some people do claim to be writing on that emotional level with easy regularity; first of all I don't think it's a good idea even to try, and in the second place I don't really believe it's possible to achieve such a thing effectively. I would dare to suggest that if we were claiming to write in such a way we would believe we were capturing deep emotion but in fact only mimicking it.

When poetry becomes too easy

A famous poet once said that we should beware when the writing of poetry becomes too easy. You might well roll your eyes at that – I certainly did when I heard those words for the first time. Surely we should celebrate when poetry flows from the pen? Half the time we lament the onset of writer's block and now at last the words are there!

If a piece of work that has been trapped in your head suddenly begins to run like a river then that indeed can be – and should be – exciting and positive. Often in such moments our subconscious frees us from all the conventions and rules and clichés of everyday language engrained in us since childhood, allowing us to pour out dynamic, vivid and original ideas and images. So, there are exceptions to the gloomy warning of that gloomy poet.

But I have to say that I think I know what he meant nonetheless. We must certainly beware when we write like this all the time. It's at that point we need to stop and take a very severe look at what we are writing and ask ourselves (and others) if we have lost our direction. That's something that can happen to the best of writers, and poets are no exceptions. Perhaps we may have started to write about one subject area too much and it is all becoming too simple. Perhaps our style has become too prosaic and needs to be challenged.

Here are some suggestions to avoid becoming stale:

- When you're tired of reading the work of one author then read that of another. If you have just attempted a Victorian poet then why not try a classical one; if your last book was by a thoroughly contemporary poet from England then read the work of a German poet in translation.

- There is a whole world of poetry to draw on – if you don't buy the books then borrow them from a local or a city library. Second-hand bookstores are by and large full to the brim with poetry volumes; find your nearest one and spend magnificent hours buried under dusty tomes. And ask the person who runs the place for titles you're on the hunt for. Reading all this work will show you what devices individual poets use, what sound worlds they create, what subjects they broach.

- Challenge yourself by writing practice poems about topics that you wouldn't normally choose; if you love describing the streets and back alleys of your city then try to write about a badger or a fox. If the world you know and love is in wild country then write about a down-and-out at King's Cross. What you produce may not be worthy of great literary awards but it will keep you moving, changing, thinking, asking...

The 'write' time

All of us are individuals, mercifully. While some of us like to rise by five and have breakfast done before dawn, and are out for a jog before the postman's on his way, others of us struggle to put four monosyllabic words in front of each other before that lunch-time cup of coffee. I have a good friend who really believes his natural body rhythm would dictate that he sleep during the day and work through the night. He put this routine into practice through our university days, but as a newspaper editor he has now had to conform to usual patterns. I'm sure there are many others who would identify with his dilemma.

It isn't always easy to achieve by any means, but as writers we need to try hard to find the time of day that suits us best for creative writing. This is as true really for the production of non-fiction articles as it is for the writing of poetry. The nature of the writing is quite different, but the principle is the same.

Of course, the difference is that the first type of writing is much more mechanical and the second has to rely on the imagination and the workings of the subconscious. But conditions for all writing demand that there should be relative quiet and an absence of disturbance (the majority of us agree with this and only a small percentage really thrive on talk or music near at hand), and a writing space that is, if at all possible, ours and ours alone.

Poems, I know, will be born at the most unfortunate of moments. Like babies, they will materialise in taxis and on underground platforms, at funerals and in the middle of the night. Sometimes it's this type of poem that is the best of the lot and I am by no means trying to prevent their births. But for the ones that are slower to come, that need patient and attentive care, the creative space is the best place in which to prepare for them.

Occasionally when I am in my own creative space late at night and the telephone rings or there is a knock at the door far beyond the normal time for calls, I am so surprised I take long minutes to recover. I have been so 'far away' in my subconscious mind that it's very hard to be dragged back all of a sudden to everyday life again.

I think it advisable to treat your creative space almost as one would a room of meditation or prayer, even if you are not of a particularly religious disposition. Generally, and especially I think when you're older and more conditioned to writing, it becomes more difficult to reach your subconscious and create imaginative work. At any rate, that has been my own experience and that of other writer friends I know! The blank page and the pen on your desk can seem very daunting; there are words in your mind but they are circling furiously and aimlessly.

'You might find it helpful to have in your creative space a copy of Kalil Gibran's *The Prophet,* or a favourite anthology or collection of poetry which has inspired you in the past.'

You might find it helpful to have in your creative space a copy of Kalil Gibran's *The Prophet,* or a favourite anthology or collection of poetry which has inspired you in the past. You might also decide to build up your own personal anthology of the meditations and poems of others which you can then open and read at random to get your mind focused and your external, material worries put to one side.

It is a question of finding what I describe as the way down the lift shaft; in other words, the catalyst for firing your imaginative mind to take you from fully conscious thought to the liberation of subconscious thought.

Carry your creativity with you

All writers, not only poets, need to be aware of the possibility of inspiration striking like lightning! I know myself that lines of poetry have come to me in the middle of woods, the middle of sermons, not to mention the many occasions when they chose to materialise in the middle of the night. Nor am I going to pretend that I always had paper and pen to catch them before they fled; just as with photographs perhaps, the best ones are those you never capture.

- Have a tiny notebook to hide away with a pen into the deepest pocket of a jacket, the darkest compartment of the car.

- Even if whole poems don't fall from the pen there and then, you will have begun the process by recording ideas which can be developed later into a whole piece.

- I throw away numerous unfinished poems, but I never throw away ideas. It's always possible to come back to something at a later date and find the ending you just couldn't catch before.

I remember speaking to a poet friend of mine a couple of years ago and he was positively glowing with happiness because he had 'found' the last line to a poem he had begun many years before and hitherto had never managed to complete.

'Have a tiny notebook to hide away with a pen into the deepest pocket of a jacket, the darkest compartment of the car.'

Summing Up

- Writing is a process that demands energy and concentration – and it can't be turned on and off.

- Don't try to write four or five poems in a single day – and certainly don't give yourself specific targets.

- Challenge yourself by writing practice poems about topics that you wouldn't normally choose. Keep yourself moving, changing, thinking and asking.

- Try to find a time of day that suits you best for creative writing, and find a creative space that works for you.

- Keep a notebook with you – even if whole poems don't fall from the pen there and then, you will have begun the process by recording ideas which can be developed later into a whole piece.

- Don't throw away your ideas – they may help your creative thinking at a later date!

Chapter Three

Editing

I have to say that I believe the editing process to be just as important in poetry as the original writing of the piece. A very different procedure – but just as important.

I am constantly reinforcing this point to primary children during writing workshops in schools because generally they will complete a poem faster than it took Shakespeare to find his spectacles and then believe utterly, wholeheartedly, that they are finished.

Of course, I have no wish to curb their enthusiasm nor that of anyone burning with new coals of poetry. That inspirational process is exactly what I have delighted in discovering myself and which I want others to celebrate. As I am by nature an encourager first and foremost, I have little wish to pour ice on the fire. But there is no point being sweet and agreeable all the time – you also have to be realistic. If people are writing poetry and want to write to the best of their ability, perhaps to get their work into print, then the editing process is one that just has to be learned.

Editing is not fun, it wins no medals. Weeding is to harvesting what editing is to poetry. It is the equivalent of getting out thistles and dandelions, and wrestling with great roots of bishop's weed! But it cannot be stressed strongly enough that the process of editing in itself is simply vital.

'I throw away numerous unfinished poems, but I never throw away ideas. It's always possible to come back to something at a later date and find the ending you just couldn't catch before.'

A time and place

I very rarely edit a poem there and then, though I suppose I'm often tempted to tweak it right away. Far better to leave it in the notebook in which you first recorded it and go away and do the dishes, or better still go away to work for two whole weeks before you even bring it into the sunlight again.

Why delay editing?

I feel this is important firstly because of the whole business of the subconscious versus the conscious, the analytical. The best lyric poems are written quite fast, sometimes so quickly that they're almost like streams of consciousness creations. The subconscious has taken over, the imagination has taken wing and your mind is flying.

But wonderful as it is to write like that, because we are scribbling so quickly we often make 'mistakes'. The rhythm scheme we adopted at the outset may break in one line or may re-evolve halfway into a different pattern entirely. Verbs may be written down quickly without our being quite sure of their 'rightness', or a line may have too many adjectives and upset the balance of the remainder of the piece, and so on.

Don't get me wrong, I'm all for free-flow writing for that first stage of the poem's development, but that shouldn't be an end to it. It's akin to finding a raw precious stone in a quarry; it possesses all the qualities and colour of a gem but it needs cutting, polishing, smoothing. It's only then that the potential at its heart will be released most fully.

Sound it out

My advice is to read the poem aloud, not once or even twice, but three times.

I've already written a good deal about how I feel poetry is linked to song and sound, about how the very words of our language are built up often of onomatopoeic sounds which create vivid, evocative pictures. Somehow a lyric poem in particular is not fully alive until it has been read aloud. The vast majority of the poems that are being written today are intended as lyric poems, so most of them fit this criterion. In lyric poems, the rhythm is of fundamental importance and the words should echo with their sounds. The many little pictures should build into one whole picture, as the tiny panes of a stained glass window fit together to create a single one.

How to 'hear' your poem

- When reading the poem aloud, listen to each word carefully.

- Listen to each line carefully. Try to see each line in terms of itself and yet as part too of the overall poem.

- Think about your intentions, work out whether you do indeed want or need a certain adjective, whether that particular line is broken at just the right point, whether the pace is slowed down too much by the presence of an extra line, and so on.

- In particular, look at your first and final lines. Often these are the ones that come to me to begin with when a poem first begins to flow, and they are mightily important for the whole magic of the piece.

- Perhaps it would be true to say that the final line is of even greater importance than the first one. If a final line is truly sparkling, it will reverberate in the mind of the reader long after they have closed the book. I think even at this moment of all the poems people quote to me and I realise that it is by and large last lines they remember – lines that are imbued with pathos and with passion!

Of course, we can't always compete with the Kiplings and the Kathleen Raines of this world, but we want our poetry to be meaningful, to say something in a new way. Weigh up those first and final lines to make sure they are worth their weight in gold!

'Listen to each word carefully. Listen to each line carefully. Try to see each line in terms of itself and yet as part too of the overall poem.'

Learning the process

It's fascinating to see the editing process at work. In the cases of some world famous poets, it's possible to see the original drafts of poems (often in the form of scribbled handwriting) and then successive versions as they generally get closer to the famous pieces we all know off by heart.

I find it particularly amazing to look at the meticulous labouring of Wilfred Owen; in my opinion justifiably the best known of First World War poets. The conditions under which he was editing (apart from his time as an invalid at Craiglockhart Hospital in Edinburgh) must have beggared belief! It is interesting to note that he frequently came back to certain unusual verbs or images he had scribbled down in first drafts (the product of the workings of his inspiration and subconscious mind). It was these inspirational (in all senses of the word) first and final lines especially that eventually found their rightful places in the finished poems.

But the million dollar question is, I'm sure you'd agree, how do you know when a poem is absolutely finished? When do you stop tinkering with it and decide you can do no more? I love painting with oils and often I face the same dilemma with a canvas – is the thing done or could I put just a little more in – an extra promontory or another shaft of light or just a hint of a different colour?

Some writer friends of mine – not just poets – struggle with this problem incessantly and sadly to the detriment of their output. They work and work at the piece of writing until something interesting happens – they actually create an entirely new bit of writing. Clearly this is going too far, it is actually destructive, because in this instance the process is potentially eternal. All one is doing is creating a new piece from the old time after time after time. You must set out to retain the original integrity of your composition.

'But the million dollar question is, I'm sure you'd agree, how do you know when a poem is absolutely finished?'

- Read your work again: I think one way of avoiding allowing one poem evolving into another one completely like this is to read the original piece over and over again. Keep uppermost in your mind what it was you wanted to say, what feeling you wanted to communicate to yourself and to anyone else who might pick the poem up. If you are still happy with that goal then edit in the light of this; do not add or change substantially so as to destroy what you created. Only aim to take away what does not hold the picture you wished to convey, not what does.

- Come to an end: of course, the editing process could go on and on itself. But learn to reach a point where you are able to put down your pen, to believe that to the very best of your ability you have carried off what you intended to. Or if the opposite is the case, then learn the equally valuable lesson of being able to tear up the poem to begin the whole process again, to discard the content but to retain the integral seed of the idea until it is ready to be planted once again.

- Get feedback: it's inadvisable to seek this from people who will feel responsible for saying nice things, so cousins and maiden aunts who gave you sweeties every time they came to visit are liable to be unhelpful here.

Seeking feedback

You want honest and constructive feedback, and preferably from more than one person. The difficulty is that if one person tells you a poem's very good, it's just their opinion. But if three people you know and respect all agree with that verdict separately, you have consensus.

So do your utmost to gain detailed and constructive criticism on your poem(s) from more than one person who a) have a love and knowledge of poetry and b) will be willing to read your work fairly but to admit to worries if they believe them to be serious. The person or people involved might be former teachers, lecturers or friends who have an interest and knowledge of literature or else write themselves.

If you find yourself really stuck here (and no shame in that) then seek out a writers' group where work is circulated among members, and good, constructive feedback is provided. The other alternative is to seek such critical feedback often advertised in literary journals where freelancers agree to evaluate a certain number of poems for a fee.

The problem with this option is that you will have no knowledge of the person offering the service, and while many poets or literary professionals will do the job required both efficiently and fairly, there is little way of checking their track record or general suitability before you make contact. The journals themselves treat the offers they receive from such individuals as bona fide and will seldom have the time or inclination to check their credentials before printing the details. Essentially, you will have to take their word for the commitment and pedigree they claim to possess.

Ultimately, your goal must be to become confident at analysing and editing your own work. No one can understand or create the 'world' of your poem better than you yourself, and for that reason don't alter a piece of work just because someone or even a number of people tell you too.

You must trust your own intuition and you must be able to pour yourself so completely into your poetry that your instincts are honed ever sharper and more clearly. That takes time, but the more you write and the more you edit, the more too your confidence with this whole process should develop and grow.

Summing Up

- The editing process is as important as the actual writing of the original piece.

- Walk away from your poem – leave it for one or two weeks before you revisit it to start the editing process.

- Read your poem out aloud, not once or even twice, but three times. Listen to each line carefully and try to see each line individually and as part of the whole piece.

- Learn to know when to stop editing – you need to reach a point where you are able to believe that to the very best of your ability you have carried off what you intended to.

- Get feedback on your work. Seek this from people who will give you honest and constructive criticism – and be sure to ask more than one person!

- Your ultimate goal must be to become confident at analysing and editing your own work. You must trust your own intuition!

Chapter Four

To Rhyme or Not To Rhyme

This is probably the thorniest question of them all. Emotions run high on both sides, but particularly from the traditionalists' perspective. And in many ways one can see why – they do have history on their side! They will argue that true poetry must rhyme; modern free verse may be richly evocative and beautiful poetic prose, but it sure as heck isn't poetry itself.

The problem with all of this – which is argued most passionately and coherently – is that we are left with an assumption that poetry is because it rhymes. As I've stated before, if that's the be-all and end-all then certainly for me it makes poetry a pretty shallow thing altogether. But perhaps before dismissing the argument, we should look fairly at rhyme and see what it achieves.

'The Great Rhymers were practising their craft day in and day out until the technicalities of rhyme became absolutely second nature.'

Using rhyme

We've already examined closely the whole business of sound in poetry, and seen that both sound and rhythm are integral parts of the process. Here the ingredient of rhyme is added:

> Now the gentle waters all the myriad pools fill sweet
> And where the rushes and the blue streams shallow meet
> A cup of golden marsh blooms sweetly blows –
> 'Tis there the single aspen graceful grows.

No doubt that rhyme is of utmost significance here. It helps to inform us at once that this poem is building into a picture of tranquillity, reflection and intense beauty. The sounds of the rhyming words have been chosen to reinforce a sense of calm, grace and pastoral harmony.

Earlier on we looked at the use of both assonance and alliteration, and the purpose of their presence being linked to that of rhyme. The difference is that with straight rhyme we expect the next rhyming word and we know where it will appear, and this in turn helps greatly in building the sense of flow and rhythm. Rhyme in conjunction with rhythm acts here like the strumming of a lyre – it guides the poem and constructs the whole world of it, building it into one single, evocative stream.

The other side

That's how rhyme should work. In the pens of the Shelleys, Wordsworths and Goethes that's all very good and well, but it's important to remember that we don't live in their age! That is self-evident on one level, but the changes are really worth considering in deeper terms. The Great Rhymers were practising their craft day in and day out until the technicalities of rhyme became absolutely second nature. They also, by and large, lived in a world untroubled by the disturbance and stress our modern society experiences. Theirs was a world more aware of and in tune with nature, and it's easy to understand why that pastoral environment almost invariably played a key role in their compositions.

The industrial revolution, urbanisation and a whole new way of living and thinking changed for ever the nature of western humanity. The gun replaced horses in war, the car replaced horses on the road. The changes ushered in an age that was composed of transience, of disharmony, of questioning. Go back and look at the whole wide spectrum of the arts at the beginning of the 20th century and observe how very disturbed people were by change: millions had poured into cities, machinery had thrown countless thousands from their traditional employment, and warfare was no longer far away where the soldiers fought but potentially in the skies right overhead. Somehow, the coming of the new poetry ties in with all of that, is understandable and even a natural consequence.

That's the background, but it's important too to examine the practical obstacles to rhyme. Because we don't tend to be aware of rhyme as once we were (except in the form perhaps of children's or comic verse), it makes it much harder to compose, and it tends to make the process much more artificial.

What's the absolute core of a poem?

I would argue that it's not the rhyme or lack of rhyme but that it's rather the poem's overall purpose, message, 'journey'. If that isn't there then everything else is rather like confetti, cake and car without the bride. Imparting the 'world' of the poem is not easy – I suspect that the chief reason a poet discards so many attempts at a piece is because this primary task has not been achieved satisfactorily.

The trouble with trying to make a poem rhyme is that the writer is making that task much harder. The danger is that the writer becomes far more conscious in the end of the next rhyming word than of the poem's purpose. It's a bit like wanting and intending to go down a main road but having to turn down a tractor track instead, degree by degree. The result is bound to be frustratingly flawed for the poet because the original intention has had to be compromised for the sake of the rhyme scheme.

But I believe there are difficulties too with the very nature of a rhyme structure which have to be taken into consideration. Achieving flow in a piece of work is of real importance, and rhyme is one of the most helpful ways of building this, but the poet has to be very careful that the greatest strength in this respect doesn't become the sharpest weapon. Familiarity breeds contempt, they say, and if the reader starts to be lulled to sleep by the predictable rhyme scheme and the expected rhymes, it would all become rather pointless.

The best answer, I feel, is to ask yourself whether you feel rhyme is right for you or not. I do meet people in writers' groups – by no means all of them from an older generation – who believe passionately that this is the most natural way for them to compose. And I read examples of work that are splendidly well-crafted.

'What's the absolute core of a poem? What is its heart? I would argue that it's not the rhyme or lack of rhyme but that it's rather the poem's overall purpose, message, "journey".'

The New Formalists

The fact is that despite our increasingly urban and constantly evolving society, rhyme is enjoying a revival. (In the next chapter I'll be looking at some of the most popular forms which people are re-adopting.)

The New Formalists as they describe themselves are fed up of the road contemporary poetry has gone down. They feel that the baby has been thrown out with the bathwater, that anything at all goes in modern poetry. Just take a bit of vaguely poetic writing, chop it up a bit here and there into different lines that fits in with the natural phrasing, and serve it up on a plate marked poetry. They have a strong case to argue; the worst of contemporary poetry pays little or no heed to rhythm, assonance, half-rhyme, imagery and metaphor. It has become indistinguishable from the pop lyric, except that most self-respecting pop lyrics do pay heed to rhythm!

It remains to be seen whether the New Formalists capture the support of poetry lovers or not, but the important thing to stress for those of you determined to practise your craft in this way is that it is very much all right to be doing so! Leonard Cohen's poetry police will not come to arrest you! You have many more friends out there than you might have done 15 years ago. And that is good news.

But there will be, I suspect, a good number of individuals who could be described as switherers, who don't honestly know if their efforts in rhyme are working effectively or not.

How do you decide?

Here's something I advocate, having put it into practice myself. You know the subject of your poem and you know the mood, the 'world' you want to create to contain it. What you don't know is which form is going to be best as a vehicle for the poem – free verse or rhyme.

- Think about the mood you want to create and ask yourself if rhyme will help or hinder.

'You know the subject of your poem and you know the mood... What you don't know is which form is going to be best as a vehicle for the poem – free verse or rhyme. Think about the mood you want to create and ask yourself if rhyme will help or hinder.'

- Then I suggest simply attempting to write the piece in both forms and seeing which comes closest to your original intention and 'idea' of the poem, the one too that best captures the mood and message.

- If you can, ask two or three individuals whose opinions you value and who would give you an honest response (rather than just the response they think you want!) to which piece works best in their view. In this way, you should gain a clear idea of the response to both attempts.

- Once you have finished a rhyming piece then read it aloud many times over to 'hear' where your rhyme or rhythm scheme may have faltered, where there are too many syllables, where a particular rhyming word has been forced or simply jars, or where you have sacrificed rhyme for meaning.

- Don't be afraid of that red pen – edit and edit again meticulously and honestly. Your finished work will be all the better for it.

Summing Up

- To rhyme or not to rhyme – it has its own impressive history of debate.

- Trying to make a poem rhyme can create difficulties; the danger is that the writer becomes more worried about the end of the next rhyming word rather than the poem's overall purpose and meaning.

- Ask yourself whether rhyme is right for your poem – there is not a right or wrong answer, it's how you feel about your creation; essentially it comes down to what you think will help create your poem's mood.

- If you decide to use rhyme, read your poem aloud to hear the rhyme or rhythm scheme. Does it work? Are there too many syllables? Have you compromised the meaning?

- Don't be afraid to edit your poem – it makes for better poetry!

Chapter Five

Rhyme and Verse Forms

In this chapter, I aim to look at several possibilities for rhyming verse, but there is neither the time nor the space to exhaust all the opportunities for this.

There are many useful guides to the different verse structures that have been constructed over the centuries – visit your local library or go online for further reading. There are also suggestions in the book list.

Below are what I consider to be the highlights.

Couplets

The simplest forms of rhyme are couplets:

> *Inspiring bold John Barleycorn!*
> *What dangers thou canst make us scorn!*

These two lines are taken from Robert Burns' epic poem *Tam O'Shanter*, certainly one of the best-known rhyming narrative poems north of the border. The rhyme and rhythm patterns shown in these two lines hardly change throughout the length of the whole piece.

Burns is very careful to use as simple rhyming words as he can find so that he has as much choice as possible when it comes to finding the rhyme for the following line. In this way, he compromises as little as possible the meaning and direction of the poem – it travels in the direction he wants rather than the direction the rhyme might dictate!

A verse form with four lines where alternate lines rhyme is also familiar to most of us (often it's what we might normally associate with nursery rhymes), or else a similar four-lined stanza where lines two and three rhyme with each other as do the first and fourth lines:

Come Time, and teach me, many years,
I do not suffer in a dream;
For now as strange do these things seem,
Mine eyes have leisure for their tears…

These lines are taken from Tennyson's *In Memoriam*. This is quite compact and complicated in comparison with the more primitive nature of the form Burns chose.

It's important to consider the pace, purpose and mood of the piece you are composing when deciding on the rhythm, and on the rhyme structure. That's a process that comes naturally to many people; for others it takes hours of meticulous labour, and no doubt that was equally true for the practitioners of past centuries.

The structure doesn't need to be formal throughout:

- You may want to play games with the whole idea of rhyming and have some sections that do and others that don't.

- You may want rhyming sections to convey a certain mood; for example, you may want changes to suggest danger, fear or movement.

It's important to stress that you need to know the rules to break the rules, and it's imperative that you are aware of the traditions before you go and knock them down. There were very good reasons why Pope, Dryden, Shelley and Keats were so successful and so revered; there is a real tendency in our day and age simply to drive off in another direction with a shrug of the shoulders and an arrogant assumption that anything they could do…

Reading any one of the greats for long enough will convince the most headstrong that this is not the case. You need to know the direction other people have chosen before finding your own and making it count.

'There are several different forms of sonnets and these were developed at the time of the sonnet's heyday – during the years of the Renaissance. The main practitioners in England were Sir Philip Sydney, Edmund Spenser, Michael Drayton and a certain William Shakespeare.'

Sonnets

Sonnets have a long and noble lineage. The Italian form was developed in the early Middle Ages and the name given to the lyric poem apparently came from the Italian for 'little song' – sonetto.

40

There are several different forms of sonnets and these were developed at the time of the sonnet's heyday – during the years of the Renaissance. The main practitioners in England were Sir Philip Sydney, Edmund Spenser, Michael Drayton and a certain William Shakespeare, whose name is often linked with the English form of the sonnet. John Milton composed sonnets too, but he created his own form that differs again and is considered, therefore, a further sub-group. The various main sonneteers tended to have the honour of having their names linked with the form they were responsible for creating.

The original idea of the sonnet was that it should fall into two distinct parts – these being known as the octave and the sestet. The first part was eight lines in length and the second six, as the Latin root to both words suggests. The octave put forward a certain idea or feeling and the sestet changed direction and responded to it, gave as it were a reply.

The rhythm scheme is always the same – five feet as they are called (in other words, five pairs of syllables which create a regular stress pattern).

The easiest way to demonstrate is to show by example, and this sonnet of Milton's on the cruel loss of his sight is one of the most revered examples in the English language:

Sonnet 19 (XIX)

When I consider how my light is spent,
E'er half my days, in this dark world and wide,
And that one Talent which is death to hide
Lodg'd with me useless, though my Soul more bent
To serve therewith my Maker, and present
My true account, lest he returning chide,
Doth God exact day-labour, light deny'd,
I fondly ask; But patience to prevent
That murmur, soon replies, God doth not need
Either man's work or his own gifts, who best
Bear his milde yoak, they serve him best, his state
Is Kingly, Thousands at his bidding speed
And post o'er land and Ocean without rest;
They also serve who only stand and waite.

The break between octave and sestet is not nearly as clear as in traditional sonnet forms here; in fact there is very little sense of a break at all. The rhyme scheme we describe as a-b-b-a, a-b-b-a, c-d-e, c-d-e, and in those terms it is entirely conventional and conforms to the Italian model.

Variations in the rhyme scheme are generally located in the sestet, the second part of the sonnet. What was traditionally permitted was a c-d-c, c-d-c structure, but other poets have developed c-d-c, d-c-d forms, and Wordsworth played around with both sestet and octave parts to create a whole range of alternatives.

The Shakespearean or English sonnet is quite different in terms of its conclusion; the first 12 lines are divided into three groups of four lines and the sonnet then finishes with a rhyming couplet. The rhyme structure becomes, therefore: a-b-a-b, c-d-c-d, e-f-e-f, g-g. There is generally an attempt to maintain the break in sense between octave and sestet, but in this form there is often more stress on the final two lines of the sonnet. This couplet is intended either to sum up the whole message of the poem or else to introduce a kind of twist-in-the-tail. In many ways then, it has moved very far from the original Italian model.

Of course, there will be conservatives who insist that the only models for sonnets are the original ones, and that any deviation from this is a betrayal of the integrity of the sonnet. But what the Renaissance teaches us is that old forms may be taken and played with and changed; not for the worse, but to introduce new possibilities and vitality.

The important thing is to learn how to be familiar with and to practise the traditional form before beginning to be brave and experimenting with variations. But some tremendous modern sonnets are still composed, going to show that attempting to pour new wine into old wineskins is a tradition that is in no danger of disappearing.

'The important thing is to learn how to be familiar with and to practise the traditional form before beginning to be brave and experimenting with variations.'

The rondeau

I admit that I knew little or nothing about this verse form until I came to write this book. As with the sonnet, there are certain rules and regulations that govern its construction, but as with the sonnet these rules have evolved and there is a certain amount of freedom for the author.

The rules I'm going to deal with first of all pertain to the traditional form of the rondeau; from its name you would rightly guess that its roots are French. It's a lyric poem comprising 15 lines; the poem is split up into three verses of unequal length – the first five lines, the second four and the third six. Some practitioners use iambic tetrameter for the rondeau, others use iambic pentameter (as was illustrated in the Miltonic sonnet). This is a use of the former:

We Wear the Mask

We wear the mask that grins and lies.
It hides our cheeks and shades our eyes –
This debt we pay to human guile;
With torn and bleeding hearts we smile,
And mouth with myriad subtleties.

Why should the world be over-wise,
In counting all our tears and sighs?
Nay, let them only see us, while
We wear the mask.

We smile, but, O Great Christ, our cries
To thee from tortured souls arise.
We sing, but oh the clay is vile
Beneath our feet, and long the mile;
But let the world dream otherwise.
We wear the mask!

Paul Lawrence Dunbar.

'The traditional form of the rondeau: from its name you would rightly guess that its roots are French. It's a lyric poem comprising 15 lines.'

The complicated part of the rondeau is its 'refrain'. A small section of the first line (perhaps the first word or first four syllables or else a phrase) is repeated in the last line of the second and third stanzas. (By the way, it isn't imperative to write the three verses in separate form, they may appear unified.) What's exciting – and the great challenge of the rondeau – is to use the refrain creatively to change its sense and emphasis in the poem (just as Dunbar has done here).

The rhyme scheme is a-a-b-b-a, a-a-b-c, a-a-b-b-a-c. Not an easy one to emulate at all with such repetition of the key rhyming words, but this is the standard form and the one to meet if you're out to try. As with all of these verse forms, read as many as possible of the previous (and present) works of fellow poets to see the range of subject material.

Haiku

This is one form of verse which can turn a roomful of normally civilised human beings into tyrannical monsters. The debate over whether Europeans in particular should write the haiku according to the rules and conventions of the original Japanese model or whether we should feel free to do very much our own thing is often very loud and fierce.

The problem with the whole form of the haiku in Europe is that we have tended to view it rather sloppily. When some teachers ask their pupils to compose a haiku over the weekend, all they sometimes seem to want is a very short (probably three lined) piece of writing that has a vaguely poetic thought behind it. Now before the National Union of Teachers sues me for slander, I am not saying that this is anything like common practice. But exist it does, and in writers' groups as much as in school or anywhere else, simply because there is confusion over the basic rules.

As with the other strict verse forms in this chapter, it's important to learn those rules before deciding that they're there to be broken.

To start off with there was originally a very real religious purpose behind the composition of the haiku, this being Zen Buddhist. There is a sense in which the masters of the form are trying to teach us something in their work; impart a sense of the moment, of change, of enlightenment. Inspiration from the seasons in particular was seen as crucial, and technically a haiku that doesn't touch on some aspect of the seasons at all was a senryu, a Japanese form of short poetry similar to the haiku.

But before all this becomes a little too complex and we start straying from the original path, let's make clear what a haiku is rather than what it isn't. There are three lines to each, and the idea is that it should be composed of 17 syllables, these arranged in a 5-7-5 pattern over the three lines.

Basho, a 17th century Japanese poet, is revered as one of the great masters of haiku.

> *The temple bell stops –*
> *but the sound keeps coming*
> *out of the flowers.*

Even here we might well describe the end of the poem as possessing a twist-in-the-tail. Our expectation is a description of the echo coming from the bells themselves or from something directly associated with them, but this third line turns everything on its head. There is also something very spiritual and almost worshipful about the linkage of the two elements.

Haikus are still being composed very widely in Europe today, whether they pay attention very strictly to the original tradition or else choose their own contemporary direction. It's important to take on board the original spirit of the form but to remember too that the conditions in which the original form was created are not part of our time or cultural experience.

If you become a devotee then watch out for competitions of the writing of haikus and even new anthologies seeking the best of recent compositions.

The ballad

Earlier in this book I touched on ballads when looking at lyrical poems in general. They were often epic, heroic tales of brave deeds completed in the face of enormous danger.

Song, poem and story become blurred when one deals with the ballad tradition because often there is something of each at work.

'If you become a devotee then watch out for competitions of the writing of haikus and even new anthologies seeking the best of recent compositions.'

What was important about the majority of the ballads was that they were about ordinary people accomplishing extraordinary deeds. This was of fundamental importance because the people listening to the ballads – or reciting them – were ordinary too.

Ballads had the possibility, therefore, to empower people, to inspire in them the confidence to believe that their lives could be better, that they could win the love they dreamed of or achieve the life they yearned for. As well as that, they were about wishful thinking, about nothing more than dreaming in the midst of a humdrum life that involved fetching and carrying and being afraid of poverty or the sword.

What came later are what are termed street ballads. These are a more recent departure, composed after the old ballads had served their time and were being a little overlooked in a new age. Street ballads tend to be more comic than heroic in tone and their heroes have the habit of possessing fairly large feet of clay. But that's not necessarily the case; a street ballad might be praising, for example, the heroic actions of striking miners who refuse to give up their struggle for rights no matter the odds. The ballad may go out of its way to highlight their ordinariness, but in doing so it weaves an even stronger web of genuine heroism about their words and actions.

Oscar Wilde's *The Ballad of Reading Gaol* comes into this category. His hero is a condemned man who, with his fellow inmates, is bravely struggling on to win dignity and freedom of spirit in the midst of the appalling prison conditions of 100 years ago.

> *As Alwyn Benn put down his ale*
> *The police began to close*
> *And though his courage didn't fail*
> *He trembled as he rose.*
>
> *The boy named Smullion sneered at Benn*
> *He mocked his filthy hands.*
> *"D'you know these hands have carried men*
> *Half dying from the stands?"*
>
> *D'you know that forty years of mine*
> *Lie coal-black in that land,*

'The majority of the ballads were about ordinary people accomplishing extraordinary deeds. This was of fundamental importance because the people listening to the ballads – or reciting them – were ordinary too.'

Need2Know

And you can only laugh, you swine,
And never understand!"

Smullion hit him hard as rock
A right hook cracked his head.
Yet Alwyn fell as much with shock,
He rose with fists like lead.

From *The Ballad of Alwyn Benn*.

The a-b-a-b, c-d-c-d pattern is not easy to maintain, as I found all too quickly when I decided to put the story outlined in the last paragraph into verse form! Even in those few lines, I had to compromise once or twice to find the rhymes I required, and it would have taken many hours to complete the whole ballad.

But there's a timelessness about the form that makes it tempting, whether for comic or deadly serious purposes. Street ballads have a tendency to be accessible, and that counts for a very great deal in an age where poets are often denounced for being deliberately obscure and intellectually arrogant. In that sense, the street ballad has not lost the original core of the original concept; it is for the people and tells their story.

Summing Up

- Learn the rules of the different verse forms before you try to break them.

- The simplest forms of rhyme are couplets.

- The original idea of the sonnet was that it should be made up of two parts: the octave and the sestet. The first part was eight lines in length, the second six.

- The rondeau is a lyric poem made up of 15 lines and is split into three verses of unequal length.

- The haiku is made up of three lines, composed of 17 syllables arranged in a 5-7-5 pattern.

- Ballads were often epic, heroic tales of brave deeds – song, poem and story became blurred. Later came 'street ballads' which are more comic than heroic in tone.

Chapter Six

Building a Poem

The elements of poetry writing

I decided to choose one of my poems to draw together the many strands I've mentioned in connection with building a poem. I've used something of my own not because I am shamelessly narcissistic, but because I know better than anyone the intentions behind my own work!

The Wind and the Moon

The wind woke me, the loud howl of it
Boomed round the house and I felt at sea;
I fastened my eyes and was out in a ship
Ten miles of Atlantic. I went to the window,
Watched the whole round of the moon
Ploughing through clouds, a coin
Of silver and gold.

All night I was blown between dreams,
Never slept deep, was thinking
Of the trees crashing and rising with wind,
Of the chestnut rain that would fall
By the morning.

At dawn I woke up, went out
Into the bright blue whirl of the wind,
Rode the wild horse of it upwards
Into the wood and beyond,
To the hill with the chestnut trees,

The leaves dancing at my feet,
Russet and gold.

I ran and ran till my chest
Hurt with my heart. Under the hands of the chestnuts
That waved and swung in the air,
Saddles of leather, polished and shining,
Broken from the beds of their shells –
A whole hoard.

I went home in a gust of light
My pockets and hands
Knobbled with conkers.

'There are many literary devices at work in the one piece and for that reason it makes the poem an interesting jigsaw puzzle to unravel and play with.'

There are many literary devices at work in the one piece and for that reason it makes the poem an interesting jigsaw puzzle to unravel and play with. I chose it too because I've used it on many occasions in both primary and secondary classrooms, as a stimulus for children to attempt to compose memory poems of their own. It's a process that draws on powerful emotions to bring to life a place, a time, a person or a combination of these elements.

- Line length

The lines are generally short, but the pattern is ragged and intentionally broken. This is because I wanted to heighten the sense of 'blowiness' in the poem; I was keen that the reader should feel physically blown through the piece from beginning to end.

The pace is relentless, the actual sentences themselves long, and with the broken, fragmentary nature of the phrasing that also helps to contribute to what I wanted to be a helter-skelter effect. I use this 'run-on' line a good deal here; this being where a line is broken at the end but actually continues sense-wise into the next – the very first two lines are an example of this.

You could generally say that to create a placid and unthreatening descriptive scene it would be most effective to have longer lines, each of which was complete and did not use a run-on pattern, though it goes without saying that it would be possible to use the latter technique sparingly.

- Mood

The intention is to build up a mood of excitement – I hope anyone reading the poem will be aware of this from the outset! Just prior to writing this poem, I had been working in a rural primary school and I asked the head teacher what she and her staff found affected the children most in terms of making them excitable. She told me at once that it was two things – the wind and the moon. That triggered off a vivid memory of when I was a youngster counting the hours until dawn returned and I could reach the best of the chestnut trees to find blown-down treasure before any of my classmates. I realised that the full moon and the wind had had an effect on me too!

From the very outset, it was my intention to build a poem around the central emotion and idea of excitement – tension and huge anticipation – that was the 'world' of the poem. The language I chose to use had to be full of dramatic, forceful, dynamic sounds – hard even. An adjective like 'whole' isn't actually really needed in the first stanza, but I think it does exactly what I'm trying to stress here, it's reinforcing the punch of the poem's pace and mood. This is so important, and for every mood and atmosphere there are different nuances which can be found, different touches with sound and style that help to communicate to the reader as nearly as possible the original feeling.

- Power verbs

I have touched on the importance of verbs before, but I want to mention them here once more since their presence is vital. The vast majority of the power verbs here – almost all of them begin with plosive, aggressive syllables – make their appearance at the beginning of lines.

This helps in two ways. The beginning of any line is its powerhouse – it's the strong end. So having strong power verbs there makes them count for even more, and in the context of the poem that's very important indeed. But the power verbs also help in terms of blowing the whole poem along, scudding the words on, jostling and jockeying for position before another bang, and the next line begins.

- Imagery

There are three particular uses of imagery here that I feel are of real importance. Firstly, the idea of being out in a ship in the opening stanza. Secondly, the picture of the wind being like a wild, unbroken stallion. Finally, the description of the chestnuts themselves being like saddles of leather.

Once again, the very sound and sense of these was designed to create suspense, excitement and wonder. I think it's all but impossible to make someone else know when and how to use imagery at all – one can only show by example.

While there is a sense in which the imagery here was planned – in that it was contributing to and boosting the existing picture – there is also a strong sense in which it worked its way naturally into the poems and was very much uncontrived. I think being able to do that has a great deal to do with the next point.

- Being there

I chose this poem as an example because it concerns a real memory, one of the most powerful I have in my mind from childhood days.

When I wrote this, I felt absolutely there again; I could hear those branches lifting and crashing beyond the window, I could scent the early morning, see the blue through the torn clouds, and I could feel those newly-fallen chestnuts. In a very real way, I was there again.

Here the experience of writing poetry all but borders on the mystical and supernatural, for in an instant like this, revisiting the place of the memory is almost an out-of-body experience.

Of course, you are not really there, but with all your senses, with your imagination and with your heart, you are breathing, feeling and drinking the full power of that memory.

- Rhythm

Although the pace of the rhythm is pretty constant throughout, I have played one or two tricks with it.

I mentioned that I wanted the reader to feel literally blown from beginning to end so that they are caught up in the same adrenaline rush of excitement as I experienced that morning. But the longest line of the poem (line 21) is designed to make the reader slow down.

The reason for this is simple; there has been a mad run up the hill to reach the chestnut tree, but now the run is over. The first one and a half lines of that stanza are all written with monosyllabic words; this is the climax of the run and I want the words themselves to sound like the hammering of a heart. But then comes the change, the break. The search has begun now, already, and the actual race to get there in time is over. So things In real life have slowed, and that's mirrored in the line. I slow the reader down by continuing the line after the full stop; if I had wanted the pace to remain the same, I would have broken the line instead.

It's fun but also very worthwhile to practise techniques concerning the creation, breaking and changing of rhythm.

Remember that it's an important way of creating tension, of lulling readers into what might be a false sense of security, or of keeping them in suspense.

■ Structure

In a sense, each new stanza deals with a separate piece of the story. I think it would have been too much if there had been no breaks at all throughout, it would have become exhausting and frustrating.

The breaks become a little akin to pauses for breath, and they are also presenting new pieces of action, changes of time and/or location. When editing this particular poem, I read it aloud up to a dozen times before I was satisfied. I wanted line endings to be just right, alliteration and assonance (not too much and yet enough to make an impact), imagery and adjectives.

At the same time, I had no wish to edit the poem to such an extent that I destroyed the mood of drama and excitement I had set out to create. I will still change individual words or phrases in the future if I begin to question them.

The editing process is never truly finished to my mind; there is always the possibility of improvement.

Summing Up

- Building a poem involves combining literary devices – structure, line length, language, power verbs, imagery, rhythm – with mood and emotion.

- Practise these techniques.

- Read your poem aloud several times.

- Don't be afraid to edit.

- Pick up an anthology from your local library and have a go at breaking down and analysing the literary devices at work.

Chapter Seven

Writing Exercises

Practice in poetry

It's important that at all stages of development as poets we should practise our craft. It's like sharpening a knife; if you leave it lying around and don't take care of it, it will go blunt. Poetry is like any craft or skill, it's mostly honest, ordinary labour. There is a sprinkling of gold dust there too (at least that is the hope!), but that makes up only 2% of it. The poets who go round with sweeping caps and an arrogant swagger are pretending the gold dust constitutes 98%.

Practice in poetry can be had in the context of writers' groups. Generally, a topic is chosen and members write their compositions either within the context of the meeting or else in the quiet of their own homes for the following get together.

But in all honesty, someone who is truly committed to writing poetry shouldn't need the formal structure of a writers' group in order to produce poems. Often writers' groups are places where people who would quite like to write, hide because they can talk about it with others without actually getting down to it!

This breakdown of ideas for finding new inspiration and developing individual paths is by no means exhaustive. You will find your own ways of working once you have discovered what writing paths are going to be of most fascination and of greatest satisfaction to yourself.

Town mouse, country mouse

Most of us are either drawn to busy streets or else to country lanes; just occasionally you will find people who are equally happy in both. Whichever you decide to inhabit – or have to live in for one reason or another – can prove a source of inspiration for poetry. The great Edinburgh poet, Norman MacCaig, divided his life between his native city and the wilderness of western Sutherland in the Highlands. It's interesting to see how MacCaig used both locations equally during his writing life to describe totally different characters and locations and events.

The point is that strong environments bring up in us humans powerful emotions, and if one thing is true of all poets then it must be that they feel things deeply and are strongly sensitive – almost more sensitive than the people who surround them. (By sensitive I don't necessarily mean caring and thoughtful. Some of the worst examples of humanity who have been great poets have lived anything but caring and thoughtful lives, especially in terms of their relationships with others.) I mean impressionable, vulnerable and aware of pain. At times, as in the case of the magnificent poet John Clare, it can drive them to the edge of madness.

'I think it's also important to get to grips with your own writing environment in writing terms because it's often the place we most overlook.'

Your own writing environment

I think it's also important to get to grips with your own writing environment in writing terms because it's often the place we most overlook.

In schools, I'm constantly begging teenagers to try to write about the tales their grandfather told them or the ship that ran aground on their local coast instead of trying to describe the middle of a park in Los Angeles or a brawl in downtown New York. The assumption is that there is no possible contest between the former and the latter as far as excitement is concerned, but even if that were true (and I don't think necessarily it is), it certainly doesn't mean that the more exotic location is the one that's going to work best in terms of their writing.

Describe what you know

Familiarity breeds contempt, but it also provides a density of experience and colour. The place where you learned to swim for the first time, where you kissed your first sweetheart, where you ran home through the warm spring rain the evening that goal was scored, where you heard the story of the building where the ghost cried on New Year's Eve, and so on.

This rich tapestry of our lives is the stuff of which poems and stories alike are made. The more we find the place we know best, the more we dig into it and explore its stories and listen to its people, and the more gold we will have in our hands and pens with which to work.

A notebook and all our senses

Go out one day with a notebook, though don't feel pressured to write anything there and then. Go first and foremost to absorb, for it was Wordsworth who knew all about recollection in tranquillity and not attempting to force experience into creative work immediately.

Go into the nooks and crannies of the place (as long as that does not lead you into open danger!) and try to be there in as timeless a way as possible. By that I mean that you see behind the walls of the place – or its trees and hills – to the people who were there before.

Be open to the past as well as to the present; allow your memory to be jogged by the stories which your own mind creates and imagines. (Seamus Heaney wrote a series of tremendous and haunting poems concerned with Stone Age people whose real graves had been opened; he then imagined the stories of their lives and deaths. The best of these are contained in his selected poems.) In writing these accounts he brings them vividly and hauntingly to life.

Above all, try to use all of your senses when you are absorbing your chosen place: listen to its noises, scent its smells and hear its sounds. Wherever possible, bring these references to the other senses and the messages about the place they give you into the poem. I stress this because in everyday life we are most aware of the information transmitted to us via our eyes. As a result, it's of little surprise that we focus on visual information when we're writing descriptively. Our creative work can be much more evocative and startling, therefore, if we refer to the sounds, the scents and the feel of the landscape in which we are, whether urban or rural. It goes without saying that this has to be practised subtly and sparsely, not done to death.

Objects old and new

Another exercise for writing poetry can be to look at an object and tell its story, either real or imagined.

I have found this of particular value in primary schools where youngsters' imaginations are as active as taps – turn them and in seconds they are flowing and alive. I think it's often harder for us cynical and staid adults to allow ourselves to be so liberated with our creativity; we've become generally too used to the facts and figures of secondary school and the big wide world beyond where what counts is rational thought, efficient calculation and unimaginative work output.

Creativity in general, whether as a catalyst for prose or poetry, means re-entering that original world of the imagination without shame. It's a childhood world, not a childish world. That's a very vital difference. Just give young children some simple objects to play with outside and they will transform them to a numberless range of imagined creatures.

I remember using a simple couch as a house, a train, a space rocket, a ship and a desert island. Even in the poorest and most deprived corners of our world, young children will transform the rudimentary sticks, stones and mud at their feet into things of magic just with one wish of their imaginations. It's that world I want us as poets to dream of reaching back to.

Here are some of the objects I use in primary classrooms, for they are as valid to the adult community as to their junior counterpart:

- A traveller's kettle.

- An old shoe.

- A smooth, green pebble from the beach.

- An alarm clock whose face is broken and that has stopped at 9.10pm.

'Creativity in general, whether as a catalyst for prose or poetry, means re-entering that original world of the imagination without shame. It's a childhood world, not a childish world. That's a very vital difference.'

- An ancient fountain pen.

It may sound as if these have been chosen entirely at random, and certainly there is no doubt that the list could be expanded upon with ease, but each is deemed appropriate because of the potential link with the human community.

The children are given a few minutes to sit in complete quiet to observe the objects and think about them. I ask them in particular to imagine the human beings who might have possessed them, whose lives were entwined with them.

- Who was it that last filled the kettle and where were they at that moment?

- Whose foot was it that fitted the shoe – that of a princess or a beggar, or was it their own brother?

- Who found the stone and why were they on the beach at that particular time?

- Was it for a particular reason that the clock stopped at that moment?

The only limit on these answers is the power of their own imaginations, and I have had the most wonderful and magical responses.

The shoe has belonged to both a refugee and a princess, the green stone has been a wizard's and the kettle was lost when the traveller family was forced to give up their way of life to live in the city. The exciting thing is that there are no right or wrong answers, only better or poorer ones, and there is certainly no end to the scope of the 'solutions', of the richness and the range of them.

For the adult groups with which I work, there are many opportunities to narrow the perimeters somewhat. I ask them to view the objects as gateways to memories of their own; a candle might bring back memories of a grandparent's house during the blackout, a child's shoe could be the story of the drowning of a neighbour's child during the summer. It opens the way to a releasing of powerful memories that might have lain latent in the mind for countless years until that moment.

Now, it's your turn:

- Take something familiar to you, or something you find on a woodland path or in a junk shop in Camden Town, and let its story take you away on a magical journey.

- Be limited by nothing except the scope of your own imaginative powers – and be determined to expand these too.

Diary poems

I find that poetry is often provoked by journeys to new places. The poems don't always grow from the pen during the journey itself or necessarily at the journey's end – more often the distillation process begins then, and once I am back home again the various new images and thoughts unite one by one.

I've never kept a diary for any length of time, but I suppose the nearest I've come to doing so is when I write what I would describe as diary poems. Somehow that label for what they are seems a little shallow and mundane, mostly because I think it makes such poems sound as if they are emotionless. The opposite is true; in drawing on all the tiny details of a particular time and place, I want first and foremost to capture all the emotion that filled me at that moment. The idea is that I should be able to come back to that poem again and again throughout my life and on reading it experience just the same feelings of elation, melancholy, fear and so on.

'It is the little tiny details – the pieces of kindling – that count for so much. As the sounds should be part of the whole framework of feeling you are trying to create, so the details should be too.'

As I have mentioned before, it is the little tiny details – the pieces of kindling – that count for so much. As the sounds should be part of the whole framework of feeling you are trying to create, so the details should be too.

An example

I'm going to use the example of a diary poem I composed very recently. I was visiting a friend on her home island in the Hebrides, and on the day I left the weather closed in from the west. I started to have one or two ideas for a possible poem, and I knew that I wanted this whole feeling of the closing in rain and the oppressively grey skies to be echoed throughout. I felt a sense of the end of summer and the melancholy that that brought, the feeling that now before us lay the long march towards winter.

An idea of the whole tone of the poem had been established, and it was that feeling – the one I'd had on the little ferry coming home – I now wanted to touch as deeply as possible in what I wrote:

The morning drums its fingers on the windows
So the glass is left shiny with crying;
Outside the rain feels like thick wool.

There is nothing to separate sea from sky –
Mull has been swallowed in a single gulp,
A ship booms somewhere like a sad whale.

Two small boys scatter puddles with flat feet;
A motorcycle like an insect intent on stinging
Hums by and becomes a thing of the past in mist.

The ferry leaves the island behind a white furl:
Red houses, a jetty, and a huddle of humans –
They are all washed away with the last of the summer.

It's interesting to point out first of all that the line which made me get out paper and pen to begin with was the one about Mull being swallowed by mist! I liked that idea of those huge skies being like some extraordinarily large creature that could eat up islands whole. I wanted to continue that idea of things and people just disappearing (and almost ceasing to exist) because of the thickness of mist and so I mention the ship that isn't there, the vanishing motorcycle, and then even the people on the island who in a rather different way – because of times and journeys – are washed away with the summer.

It is a diary poem, but it isn't an entirely truthful one, for quite a lot of poetic licence has been employed! The two small boys were real, but I saw them on another day entirely. I have to confess that the ship far out in the Atlantic was nothing more than a fictitious addition which struck me as adding to the whole feeling of the oppression of the storm clouds and their anthropomorphic quality.

Each of the different verses represents a slightly different picture, and also a progression. I think I might compare that to four different paragraphs in a diary account.

- The first is an impression of the world from inside; it sets the scene and at the same time it introduces a progression. By the end of the first verse/stanza, the narrator has gone out into this world for real.

- In the second, the impressions are very much of the distance; they are undisturbed by any other presence.

- By the time the third comes, however, there is perhaps a sense that time has moved on and the place is becoming busier; the relationship is no longer only between the narrator and the environment but with other people too, even if only on an impersonal level.

- There is no doubt what the fourth concerns; this stanza introduces the greatest change of all, and also draws the threads of the poem as a whole together to round it off, to state its message and its deepest emotions.

So evolution within a poem of this kind is of fundamental importance. Even if not a great deal happens, there should be a sense of progression, of movement, of journey.

I think diary poems show – as well as much else – just how very much may be imparted in a mere handful of lines.

The spark of other people's fires

I have stressed before and will stress again the importance of other people's poetry. I mean writing we could describe as great, whether ancient or comparatively recent. To understand how poetry moves us, when it does and in what ways is half the battle of learning how to do it ourselves. It is the easy half, I think, but it's a very important half nonetheless.

I know myself that on occasion (generally at night and in bed) I will pick up a copy of the selected poems of Seamus Heaney, Wilfred Owen or Walter de la Mare and read something that strikes a chord within me. It will transport me to somewhere of my own in a very vivid second, and set my memory racing about something partially related to the original poem or else absolutely unrelated to it. Now and again I will reach for paper and pen even before I've finished reading!

I remember once at university coming across one of Seamus Heaney's early poems concerned with picking potatoes. I had done that same task (most unwillingly) as a boy at school in Perthshire, and into my mind there flew a whole host of images like black crows that conjured up the wet autumn fields, the travelling people, the arthritic tractor, the look and the feel of the potatoes, and so on. It certainly didn't mean that I was copying Heaney's original – I was being inspired by the spirit of his poem rather than the form.

It's very important to differentiate between those two things. There's no use in producing a pastiche of a famous poem and trying lamely to pretend yours is original. This does become difficult if you are blessed (or perhaps burdened might be nearer the mark) with a very good ear. By that I mean that you find yourself imitating some author's work unconsciously because you are so familiar with its rhythm and vocabulary. I know myself that whenever I try to write anything at all that deals with warfare, I inevitably start to sound far more like Siegfried Sassoon or Wilfred Owen than anyone else, far less than myself!

This is something you will have to be tough on yourself with. Have the courage to scrub an effort if you find that your voice is being suppressed by that of the other author.

But try the exercise. Read the work of one of your favourite poets and be inspired by something of theirs. Let it make you think of a situation, place or event of your own and put the original poem away while you compose your piece.

I think this is a particularly good exercise to choose if you're suffering from writer's block at the time. All of us experience times of stagnation creatively and need to take stock of our direction to know where to go next.

- Read your chosen poet's work determined to be challenged by the way he/she approaches language, imagery, form and so on.

- Ask yourself what new things you can learn from him/her stylistically. See how different techniques are effective and for what reason.

You don't necessarily need to keep the poems you compose in the wake of reading the original poem that inspired you. Sometimes it will be too derivative; sometimes you will be trying too hard. But it's an exercise that can turn up nonetheless some inspiring results.

Just think of one of the most famous examples, Keats' *On First Looking into Chapman's Homer*. That's the kind of fire we want to find!

'Read the work of one of your favourite poets and be inspired by something of theirs. Let it make you think of a situation, place or event of your own and put the original poem away while you compose your piece.'

Summing Up

- Practice is important to the development of your work.

- Describe what you know – draw on your experiences and surroundings.

- Take a notebook with you – you don't have to make notes, but encourage yourself to absorb the people and places around you.

- When you've chosen a particular focus, use your senses: listen to its noises, scent its smells, hear its sounds and so on.

- Look at an object and tell its story, either real or imagined.

- Write down any details that inspire you – build up a poetry diary. This can be drawn on for inspiration at a later date.

- Read the poetry of others and let yourself be inspired. Let it make you think of a situation, place or event of your own and put the original poem away while you write your own.

Chapter Eight

Writing to Heal

Why do we choose poetry?

If you were to ask everyone in your community to compose a poem and you were to sift through the resulting work analysing the topics chosen, I bet my bottom dollar that half – if not more – would be cathartic poems about the deaths of famous media icons and revered people, or about terrible world situations that had received much television coverage.

Many individuals who would never normally dream of writing poetry find themselves doing so either in the wake of a personal loss – the death of a loved one in particular, or the collapse of a relationship, or because of a major traumatic event in which they or someone close to them has been involved.

There is nothing wrong with this, indeed there is everything right about it! But why is it that people choose poetry so frequently? Because poetry is about condensed emotion, hard-packed feeling. Generally, it says in a few evocative and lyrical lines what a short story or a drama would have taken pages to impart.

That's why the Celtic countries are so full of haunting songs that record the tragedy of battles, of lost loves and so on. The bards – the poets of that time who accompanied themselves on harps – composed verses that were both songs and poems at one and the same time. Those songs were easy to remember for a people who relied on a totally oral tradition, and so they were passed down from grandmother to mother to daughter and so on.

However, it goes to show that although the nature of our tragedies has changed – we now mourn those who are dying in wars half a globe away, or remember the sacrifice of leaders in countries that were not even known to the Celts – the need to express grief, loss and pain remains just as important.

Yes, such writing can be very healing. Sometimes I read a poem that someone may have written on the circumstances of Diana's death and I wonder just why they have put pen to paper. What has it achieved? I don't need to ask why someone pours out their grief over the death of a loved one, or the loss of a beloved partner or friend, but it seems a particular feature of the television age to write in mourning over the death of a media icon the person hasn't ever met.

But quite why this is possible is another question entirely. What matters is that the writer, I think, feels afterwards a little like the person who left some flowers outside Kensington Palace in that great sea of blossom and tributes. They feel they have said goodbye in person, in their way, and that is what matters.

I don't want to prevent anyone from writing like that. I do want, however, to suggest one or two ways in which this writing for healing might be tackled differently, and I hope more usefully. The problem with composing something for a distant and unknown person is that we don't have the detail – and therefore the depth – to make such a poem truly effective.

The imagination can be used in a most powerful way to make a remote situation or individual come vividly to life. One of the most moving examples I can offer is of a beautifully haunting poem written about the captain of the Titanic. He has survived the disaster, not drowned, and he is thinking back in agony on that fateful night. The emotional impact of the poem is heightened because the narrator has written the piece in the first person – imagining, in other words, that he is the captain himself.

It is further brought to life because of the use of very effective kindling; tiny (mostly imagined) details of the captain's memories and existence which assist in building up a truly vivid and magnificent portrait of a man whose life has been shattered utterly. I suspect that it was probably because of the effect of this on me in school days that I wrote many years later a poem dealing with the haunted memories of the pilot of the Anola Gay – the pilot who dropped the bomb on Hiroshima.

I admit that it may be more difficult to write such faction – a mixture of fiction and fact – the closer one is to a tragedy, either personal or universal. But what I want to suggest is that we attempt to role-play here so as to get as close as possible to the emotions involved.

Right now as I work on this chapter over a hundred Russian sailors may be trapped alive on a submarine in the Arctic Ocean. Every hour or so I think of them and imagine myself with them, experiencing the inexorable fading of hope. I want to write something from the perspective of one of them, imagining their life, their thoughts as they face near certain death, their vision of those around them. I don't want to do this voyeuristically or sensationally, I want to do it because I actually want to attempt to feel something of their pain. If I write a poem as a distant observer in Scotland then what impact will that have? What will it serve to show except detachment? The only kind of poem then that would work in that context would be something dealing with the frustration of detachment.

What about the day of the Omagh bombing? The suffering of a parent whose child has vanished as the terrible wait for news goes on and on and on. Or, what about 9/11? The suffering of a wife or husband who has lost a partner in the destruction.

I think this attempt to get right under the skin of someone's suffering is important because as human beings we are linked by our humanity. All of us will face loss and bereavement and fear, even if not in the kind of appalling measures suffered by those who endure the tragedies I've outlined above.

Poets are deeply aware of pain, of emotion in all its rawness, and feeling it – not running away from it – is a vital part of becoming wiser, stronger and more able to empathise.

Write about your own suffering, your neighbour's suffering, the suffering you see every night on television. But use your imaginative powers to get under the skin of it, to come close to it, to feel it as if it were your very own.

Individuals not groups

Let's say that you are moved by the plight of many millions of starving people in sub-Saharan Africa. So moved that you decide you have to write about them and for them, a poem that gets out from your system the pent-up frustration and confusion you feel at their suffering. How do you best tackle such a subject?

'Poets are deeply aware of pain, of emotion in all its rawness, and feeling it – not running away from it – is a vital part of becoming wiser, stronger and more able to empathise.'

The irony is that it's very difficult, if not utterly impossible, to write about collective suffering in a way that captures the emotion of the situation. What sort of picture do we get in our heads when we imagine 10 million starving people? Probably no picture at all, because it's inconceivable, it is something none of us has encountered.

The only poet I know who has managed to achieve the task successfully (though I have no doubt there have been others) was the most famous post-war Polish poet. He had lived through the horror of Auschwitz, the most notorious of all the Nazi concentration camps, and he wanted to come to terms with something of the suffering of the Jewish people en masse, particularly those who had died in Auschwitz. The problem is, as I have stated, that talking about the deaths of millions, no matter how appalling those deaths may have been, cannot have a real effect on the human psyche. It has to be imaginable, not unimaginable. What the poet did was to describe a pile of all the shoes that had belonged to the Jews of the camp, nothing more than that. It is moving and effective because there is a focus for our emotions, it is no longer diffuse and invisible.

That was one solution and doubtless there have been others. Let us come back to the analogy of the starving children (though we might just as well think of the Auschwitz illustration too in this context.) What about writing about the same plight from the perspective of just one child; capturing the memories of their mother, the longing for water, the desire to play again. Bring out their character, their loves and memories, their individuality, the dreams they had for the future. Now instead of writing about them as a distant observer, you are imagining them from within. You will make that account of the plight of all those people far more powerful by getting inside the hunger of that one child than trying to describe that famine's hugeness.

So it is that in writing in general, it is individuals who count again and again. Hence the power of the play, the novel and so on. So it is true in poetry too.

'In writing in general, it is individuals who count again and again. Hence the power of the play, the novel and so on. So it is true in poetry too.'

Writing in the midst of depression

On a number of occasions now, I've had the privilege of working with Survivors' poets. Survivors as an organisation is composed of individuals from all walks of life who have suffered from depression and who see themselves as survivors of the mental health system. They exist to encourage one another in small groups around the country, and the one thread that binds them is poetry.

Much of what members produce in the way of new writing deals explicitly with their experiences of depression, its treatment and aftermath. The whole idea is that sharing in a very real and brave way the pain and suffering of depression will firstly assist in letting go of some of the dark baggage of the poet's own memories. Naturally enough it will also serve to create solidarity with fellow sufferers.

However, groups do not just exist as gloom pools – far from it! One of the most hilarious and inspiring workshops I have ever participated in was with a Survivors' group in Glasgow. While for many it's important to deal with a past (and perhaps a present too) that's dogged by depression, it's equally valid for many to write about the rest of life and the brightness they may have found after getting over the trauma of mental health problems.

We've always known as humans that dark bouts of melancholy and great surges of creative expression are often locked into a single personality. I don't need to begin to reel off a list of names as long as my arm of great poets who were saddled also with oppressive weights of depression and self-doubt. That doesn't mean to say that it's an essential component for the composition of poetry, but the two are often bound up together and have been ever since the psalmist King David poured out his soul's pain to God in poetry so beautifully haunting it all but rends the heart.

I think it would be presumptuous of me to suggest that those readers suffering from serious depression should write in the midst of it for healing. I am fortunate enough not to know what the pain of clinical depression is really like, but I do know enough sufferers to realise just something of what it must be like to bear it.

Yet writing about depression with hindsight, once a wave has passed, that I do suggest. Name it, capture it, cage it. C S Lewis in one of his *Chronicles of Narnia* describes a dark island which a ship must pass. Fear and self-doubt make the journey a nightmare. But on the other side, once it has been passed, understanding and clarity make the dark island much less fearful and imprisoning, so that the next time it is faced it may not hold the same horror and trauma.

'Fear and self-doubt make the journey a nightmare. But on the other side, once it has been passed, understanding and clarity make the dark island much less fearful and imprisoning, so that the next time it is faced it may not hold the same horror and trauma.'

Writers' groups

I happen to feel that this is one area where the writers' group can function particularly well. By writers' group in this context I am thinking first and foremost of a group for people who feel particularly prone to psychological pain and bouts of depression, where the poetry is a means to an end, a rope by which the individuals concerned may independently and /or collectively lift themselves from suffering.

In this context, meetings themselves will be of significance, gatherings where fears may be articulated and situations discussed. We now come back to the metaphor of the dark island I used in the previous section of this chapter; for many (I would expect the vast majority), carrying the dark island alone will prove much harder and more dreadful than attempting to share it. That's part one.

But the other function of the group – the lion's share of its purpose – will be to write about pain. Not only personal suffering, but the shadows others know, or tragedies either local, foreign or universal.

- What is it really like to lose a child in an accident?

- How do people cope when they are surviving in the Philippines on an enormous rubbish dump?

- How do we conquer our inner fears and anguish over global warming?

- What would it be like to write a poem in Cuba or one of the new Russian states about political freedom and be arrested and 'disappeared' by the secret police?

All of these situations and thousands more are of importance. Why not make the ideas and questions that come out of your exchanges in the group the subject of poems? And cut to the core of these situations, imagine the people at the heart of them.

On the other side of all this, consider making a place for the good stories and the ones that made you laugh. In our society, we spend most of our time bewailing the state the world is in and very little of it being grateful for what is good.

Remember too that humour is very much the other face of tragedy. Most comedians are people who couldn't get through life at all if they weren't able to see its irony and the foolish little ways of their fellow creatures and themselves.

What to do with it all

Sometimes a particular situation, whatever it might be, will bring out truly profound poetry. Go through English literature – or that of any other language – and you'll find that to be true again and again. But what does one do with this writing? Is it acceptable to publish a very emotive poem on the abduction of a child or the suicide of a close friend? Is it right to use someone else's suffering for one's own creativity?

I heard a story recently about a poet who observed a child's terrible poverty in a developing country, wrote something about it there and then, and tore the poem up into tiny pieces as soon as it was done. He felt it would be exploitation of that child's suffering to walk away with a 'great' poem.

This has to be an individual decision for any writer, whether it be of poetry, prose or of a journalistic nature. We have to look at our writing very hard in the mirror and examine our motives. Who is the poem for? Will someone be hurt by it? What is its overall purpose?

If others are directly affected by the poem's content then it's worth considering showing it to them before you distribute it further. I was recently in this very situation and bitterly regret not having done exactly what I am now advocating. The situation taught me that different people react in very different ways to grief; one person's blessing is another's bane. Don't assume that you can predict that reaction – it isn't worth it.

Be very careful with poems that deal with identifiable local situations in particular. Poetry is so powerful; it is nothing less than emotional dynamite. Even if you try to disguise the characters involved, ask yourself just what you would do if people involved, either directly or indirectly, were to find out the truth.

If you must publish the piece then try to do so somewhere where you and the situation you describe have anonymity. If even that is too great a risk then keep the poem for yourself and yourself alone. Let it be healing for you – that's why you wrote it to begin with. With this most precious kind of poetry, it's the process that matters first and foremost and not the publishing.

Summing Up

- Writing for healing can be tackled in several ways.

- Use your imagination to make a remote situation or individual come vividly to life; write faction – a mixture of fiction and fact – and use role-play.

- Write about individuals, not groups. Get 'under the skin' of the situation.

- Use your own personal emotions to write your poetry – use your experiences and thoughts to help your individual healing process.

- Don't forget that humour is also a powerful tool.

- Be very careful with poems that are based on other people's experiences – don't assume you can predict their reaction.

Chapter Nine
Poetry for Children

First things first

I grew up with *A Child's Garden of Verses* by Robert Louis Stevenson close to my bedside. It was something I loved to pick up, whether I was ill, sad or excited. Even to this day, I can open the book and remember how I felt at some particular moment in childhood, what feelings individual poems gave me.

Writing deliberately for children can be in many ways contrived. It would not be different from setting out purposely to write specifically for women, or for a certain chosen race of people, or whatever. That's just not how poetry usually is, because inspiration to write is of itself rather than qualified in some deliberate way.

But let's think of writing for children in general terms. I have produced several stories for the picture book market and when I first started to compose such texts I think I attempted to write 'down' to that age range. I was aware of any number of similar books and I felt that my duty was to write very deliberately for the market. But rejection slips made me realise very swiftly that I was doing something seriously wrong.

Writing for the child inside yourself

If you want to write anything at all for children, whether it be drama or prose, fiction or poetry, you need to be writing first and foremost for the child inside yourself; the child that has never grown up.

Much of this draws on what I have mentioned already in terms of 'being there', of living your writing so much that you are back there with the emotions you felt at that time. Those who can be children again write the best children's poetry, who are not afraid to feel the vulnerability and the silliness of becoming seven

> 'Those who can be children again write the best children's poetry, who are not afraid to feel the vulnerability and the silliness of becoming seven once more.'

once more. In fact, many not only don't mind that regression, they positively thrive on it. In writing about that world, they can recover the safety and sheer joie de vivre of a time they loved and perhaps never quite came to terms with saying goodbye to.

Language

Many people when they first write for children – this goes for all genres and not only for poetry – worry about what language is going to be comprehensible to their readership. This is particularly true for writing for the youngest age range. Of course, it is of importance that a child doesn't stumble over a particular word or phrase in what they are reading so that they lose interest and give up. But don't put the cart before the horse. Write your text first and worry about the language you use later – it all comes back to what I wrote earlier about the inspirational part of the process versus the analytical part. Don't confuse them.

Secondly, bear in mind that new words can be of fascination to a child as well as stumbling blocks. I am aware of this now when I go back to read *Winnie the Pooh*; one or two characters in particular use language which is way beyond the comprehension of the average reader. But the words are used to clever and often humorous effect. The difficult words are by and large fascinating, and in many ways they don't terribly matter in themselves anyway.

Do be aware of the language you use, however. When editing your work, try to read the text from the perspective of a child of the age you intend it for. Think what words could be considered challenging and off-putting and be sure that in one way or another these words are 'coped' with.

Ensure that concepts are explained, terms translated and ideas put into simpler terms. Play games with language too and with big words; make them fun and exotic things rather than daunting obstacles to be feared and to run from.

This particular little comic verse scuttled into my head during a church sermon, and the final verb, though complex, works I feel within the context of the overall piece. I hope it makes the verse funnier (somehow it sounds more dramatic than 'eating') and obviously it works because of the rhyme with the final noun.

The crocodile
Takes quiteawhile
To munch
Lunch
Especially when he's consumin'
Human

Verse

I don't intend to reiterate all of what was covered in the general chapter concerning rhyme. Much of it, however, remains equally valid when considering poetry for children.

By and large, verse is what we know first of poetry as children. Rhyme and rhythm are two important component parts of that early learning process, as is the whole notion of a chorus. Just think of any nursery rhymes that spring to mind and consider how often those factors play an integral part. These rhymes help to form the building blocks of language that we will use in all the years to come.

We tend to blame teachers still for teaching only rhyming poetry to slightly older primary children in particular. While it is true that a generation or two back the bulk of what was used in classrooms was composed of classic rhyming verse (Kipling, Tennyson, Yeats, and so on), the majority of teachers have moved on to be aware of the modernists and to introduce this to pupils.

The problem often is that youngsters themselves still think in terms of rhyme in the early primary classes. Their heads are still full of those first rhymes they sang or chanted in chorus, and for them poetry does mean verse. They want more of the same! So it may be that contemporary free verse is looked upon with suspicion and dislike by the majority of them, and that the teacher will face a real battle to win hearts and minds.

However, the truth is that these two very general forms of presenting poetry don't have to be perceived as mutually exclusive, as locked in mortal combat. I'd certainly want to present a good deal of rhyming poetry to a class at that stage of primary school as well as wanting them to learn that poetry is just as

'Rhyme and rhythm are two important component parts of that early learning process, as is the whole notion of a chorus. Just think of any nursery rhymes that spring to mind and consider how often those factors play an integral part.'

much and more about rhythm as it is about rhyme. Early on too I would want them to have the chance to choose which form felt most natural to them, to experiment with both, and above all to enjoy this world of poetry as a whole.

Writing to publish

'Editors like as wide a range of tone as possible, and as wide a range of styles. They appreciate wordplay, the careful use of difficult language (for the reasons I outlined earlier in this chapter) and they will be glad to see uproarious humour cheek by jowl with melancholy.'

All this goes to show is that it is perfectly all right to be producing rhyming verse for youngsters. Many anthologies and single author collections contain work in rhyme, indeed many are all but composed of rhyme to the exclusion of anything else.

If you're serious about writing poetry for children and having your work published, then at some point go to one of the high street bookshops and browse through their children's section. Take a notebook and pen to jot down the names of publishers producing the kind of material that's akin to your own; see how many poems are used in an average publication, note their length and consider the range of topics covered throughout.

Both the anthologies and the single author collections are very eclectic in terms of content; a poem about splashing in puddles may appear alongside a verse about an elephant's trunk which in turn is printed beside a song about the orosofolus (which is plentiful in Egypt.)

Editors like as wide a range of tone as possible, and as wide a range of styles. They appreciate wordplay, the careful use of difficult language (for the reasons I outlined earlier in this chapter) and they will be glad to see uproarious humour cheek by jowl with melancholy. Different poems for different times, and as we all know children's moods swing far faster and more radically than our own.

Read your work aloud; read it and prune it, pare it down to the best it can be. Read it if at all possible to real children – your own or someone else's! Read at a playgroup, read to a primary class, to a Sunday School.

Ask youngsters to tell you what they have most enjoyed and what in turn they found boring or difficult. I guarantee you won't be short of answers; children are the most brutally honest literary critics around and they will tell you happily (and with a yawn) that your favourite, funniest poem was stupid or rubbish. Likewise, they can light up like a sunrise at something you didn't terribly value.

Take their reactions seriously; this is your audience, and what we as adults may rate, a single child or a flock of children may look upon as utterly dull, and vice versa.

It will help you bit by bit to get a picture of what works and what doesn't, what appeals to them and what is simply meaningless. Subjects of fascination, of humour, of interest to boys, of interest to girls, of interest to city kids, and so on. Ask your audience what they like – get to know them and write the poems they will want to hear and hear again.

Collections

All that having been said, this particular area of the book market is unbelievably difficult to conquer. There are any number of different publishers on the look out for picture book and junior book authors, but the number that even produce one or two anthologies or single author collections of poetry is very small – and declining.

The gloomy truth is that at present it's the latter group that's suffering most. More and more often, collections of poetry by one author are appearing from 'the usual suspects', those who have made their name generally in some other area of children's writing and whose names will be immediately familiar to their audience.

As with the adult writing world, it's not so much at times the nature of the content that counts so much as the name on the cover. This is sad and frustrating, particularly since a good deal of the 'poetry' in these collections is not of great merit at all. Indeed, some of it is really a waste of precious forest!

So how do you break into the market?

The answer is through anthologies:

- Many publishers produce anthologies concerned with different themes: horror, nature, school, humour, science fiction and so on. In fact, this is the way the market is developing at present. The best approach is to write to the editor of a certain children's division at a particular publisher and ask what material they are looking for and what anthologies are being planned.

- Ask to be put in touch with the person who is editing the anthology – often this task is done by a freelancer.

- The more you are known in anthologies, the easier it will be to approach a publisher at the end of the day to inquire about submitting a whole collection for consideration. It will require patience, diligence and sheer hard work. But then you wouldn't be keen to write poetry if you didn't know that already.

Summing Up

- If you want to write for children, you need to be writing first and foremost for the child inside yourself.

- Try to go back to your childhood, with the emotions you felt at the time.

- When editing your work, try to read the text from the perspective of a child of the age you intend it for.

- Rhythm and rhyme are two important parts of the early learning process – rhymes help to form the building blocks of language.

- If you want to get your work published, browse through the children's section in one of your local bookshops. Jot down the names of publishers producing the sort of work that you produce; note how many poems are used in an average publication, their length and the range of topics covered.

- To breakthrough into publishing, the best approach is to write to the editor of a children's division and ask what material they are seeking for anthologies and what anthologies are being planned.

- The more you are known in anthologies, the easier it will be for you to approach a publisher in the future to inquire about submitting a whole collection for consideration.

Help List

Creative writing courses, poetry courses, children's writing courses – they are all the rage in America and Britain, partly because we have never had quite so much leisure time, and retired folk in particular are leading more and more active lives. I have nothing against such courses in themselves; having read a fair percentage of the material they produce and the essay topics they set, I would say I was reasonably impressed with what I've seen.

The problem comes when people are guaranteed some kind of writing qualification at the end of the course; like everything else on the market in today's society, it all has to be quantifiable, it has to do what it says on the packet or else. But writing cannot be equated with lettuce seed or body building equipment – poetry in particular!

I take onboard the possibility of teaching someone formulaic writing, the kind of techniques that might be employed in writing certain types of genre novels, short stories or even articles. But the whole nature of poetry militates against this type of production line technique; poetry is spontaneous, works in the subconscious and is all about an automatic, undictated flow that cannot be taught and therefore cannot be learnt. Well, learnt only to the extent of each individual becoming in tune with their creative space, their deepest memories, their personal writing skills and style, their voice.

So I am sceptical of any poetry writing course that claims to teach how to produce poetry. But learning about the work of the greats, learning how they dealt with ideas, how they were inspired and began to compose – all of that is of huge relevance and value. The possibility too to establish a good one-to-one relationship with a tutor who is willing to evaluate a student's work and offer constructive criticism of it is also to be valued.

At the end of the day, I'm saying just what I said at the beginning of this book – I don't believe you can teach somebody to write poetry, but I do believe you can teach somebody to write better poetry.

I think the best solution is to approach establishments running such courses and decide yourself if this is for you. Try to glean as much information ahead of time about what is on offer before committing yourself, and preferably talk to a course leader or someone who has experience of the course at first hand. Consider too the option of taking an evening class more locally in poetry/ literary appreciation, something that when all is said and done may inspire you to write poetry just as much as a formal and more proscriptive course.

Poetry courses

The Arvon Foundation

60 Farringdon Road, London, EC1R 3GA
Tel: 0207 3242554
london@arvonfoundation.org
www.arvonfoundation.org
Offers a wide choice of courses. Use the online search facility to find poetry courses near you. A separate section included for young people. Hosts the Arvon International Poetry Competition.

Course Enquiries - Exeter Phoenix

Bradninch Place, Gandy Street, Exeter, EX4 3LS
Tel: 01392 667081
www.exeterphoenix.org.uk
Click on the 'education' tab for details of courses and workshops.

Directory of Poetry Courses

www.writewords.org.uk
Click on 'directory' and then under poetry, click 'courses.' You can also find groups, competitions, resources, magazines and news.

Literature Training

PO BOX 23595, Leith, EH6 7YX
info@literaturetraining.com
www.literaturetraining.com

Click on 'training and events' for details of workshops, courses and conferences being held across the UK by training providers.

The Poetry School

81 Lambeth Walk, London, SE11 6DX
Tel: 0207 5821679
administration@poetryschool.com
www.poetryschool.com
Offers a programme of classes to teach adults to write poetry. You can choose from one day courses, through to one year courses. There are teaching centres across the UK. Online courses are available to download too.

Ty Newydd Writers' Centre

Ty Newydd, Llanystumdwy, Cricieth, Gwynedd, LL52 OLW
Tel: 01766 522811
post@tynewydd.org
www.tynewydd.org
National writers' centre for Wales. List of courses on the website.

University of St Andrews

School of English, Castle House, University of St Andrews, Fife, KY16 9AL
Tel: 01334 462666
english@st-andrews.ac.uk
www.st-andrews.ac.uk

University of Derby

Student Information Centre, Kedleston Road, Derby, DE22 1GB
Tel. 01332 590500
askadmissions@derby.ac.uk
www.derby.ac.uk

University of East Anglia

Continuing Education Admissions Team, University of East Anglia, Norwich, Norfolk, NR4 7JT
Tel: 01603 593252
cce.admiss@uea.ac.uk

www.uea.ac.uk

University of Reading

Centre for Continuing Education, London Road, Reading, Berkshire, RG1 5AQ
Tel: (0118) 3782347
continuing-education@reading.ac.uk
www.reading.ac.uk

University of Warwick

Centre for Lifelong Learning, Westwood Campus, University of Warwick,
Coventry, CV4 7AL
Tel: 024 76524617
cll@warwick.ac.uk
www2.warwick.ac.uk

This is obviously only a very small selection of universities – check your local
university or college to see if they run poetry courses. Your local library or arts
centre should also be able to help.

Support for writers

Arts Council, England

www.artscouncil.org.uk
Championing, developing and investing in artistic experiences in England that
enrich people's lives. Supports a range of art including literature.

Contemporary Writers

www.contemporarywriters.com
This website is great if you want to search for poets to inspire you. Its database
contains up-to-date profiles of some of the UK and Commonwealth's most
important living writers. Included are writers from the Republic of Ireland the
council has worked with. You'll find reviews, bibliographies and biographies
– ideal if you're looking for fresh material to read!

Forward Press Ltd

Remus House, Coltsfoot Drive, Peterborough, PE2 9JX
Tel: 01733 890099
info@forwardpress.co.uk
www.forwardpress.co.uk
Forward Press is the largest publisher of new poetry in the world. They hold regular competitions for both adults and young writers, and selected poetry is published in anthologies. Submission themes are on the website.

Irish Writers' Centre

www.writerscentre.ie
Supports established and aspiring writers throughout Ireland. You'll find information here on workshops, lectures, seminars, writers' groups, competitions and courses.

National Association of Writers' Groups (NAWG)

PO Box 3266, Stoke-on-Trent, ST10 9BD
www.nawg.co.uk
The aim of this organisation is to bring writers' groups and individuals together. There is a searchable directory of members across the UK on the website, as well as articles and details of latest competitions and events.

The Northern Poetry Library

Gas House Lane, Morpeth, Northumberland, NE61 1TA
Tel: 01670 500390
www.northumberland.gov.uk
Holds the largest collection of contemporary poetry in England outside of London. You will find anthologies, poetry collections and magazines.

The Poetry Archive

PO Box 286, Stroud, Gloucestershire, GL6 1AL
www.poetryarchive.org
The Poetry Archive helps make poetry accessible by all. A comprehensive selection of poetry is online for you to listen to and read. Separate sections also included for teachers and students, with lots of useful resources.

The Poetry Library

www.poetrylibrary.org.uk

www.poetrymagazines.org.uk

The Poetry Library holds a comprehensive collection of poetry, and details of publishers and competitions. It's also the home of 'poetry magazines', a massive database of UK magazines (both printed and online).

The Poetry Society

www.poetrysoc.com

A charitable organisation providing information for specialists and the general public. Visit the website for details of latest events, competitions, commissions, promotions and publications. Writers can get help with their poetry here. Home of the *Poetry Review*.

The Poetry Trust

9 New Cut, Halesworth, Suffolk, IP19 8BY

tel: 01986 835950

www.thepoetrytrust.org

One of the UK's major poetry organisations, delivering a year-round live and digital programme, creative education opportunities, courses, news, events, prizes and publications.

The Scottish Poetry Library

Tel: 0131 557 2876

www.spl.org.uk

The library holds contemporary Scottish poetry, poetry from around the world, poetry for children, current magazines and back numbers – great if you're needing some inspiration! You can also read poetry online.

Society of Authors

Tel: 0207 3736642

www.societyofauthors.org

The Society of Authors provides information and advice to all writers. Today it has more than 8,500 members writing in all areas of the profession. Visit the website for news, events and resources.

Writers' Forum

www.writers-forum.com

This is a magazine dedicated to helping new and aspiring writers. Packed with the latest information, the magazine includes tips and advice from established writers, as well as experts in the publishing world. It also runs regular poetry competitions. Visit the website for further information and individual contacts.

Poetry magazines & journals

This is only a very small selection – you can search for more online yourself.

10th Muse

33 Hartington Road, Southampton, SO14 0EW
www.nonism.org.uk/muse

Acumen

6 The Mount, Higher Furzeham, Brixham, Devon, TQ5 8QY
www.acumen-poetry.co.uk

Ambit

17 Priory Gardens, London, N6 5QY
www.ambitmagazine.co.uk

Chapman

4 Broughton Place, Edinburgh, EH1 3RX
www.chapman-pub.co.uk

Magma Magazine

23 Pine Walk, Carshalton, SM5 4ES
www.magmapoetry.com

New Welsh Review

PO Box 170, Aberystwyth, Ceredigion, SY23 1WZ
www.newwelshreview.com

The New Writer

PO Box 60, Cranbrook, Kent, TN17 2ZR
www.thenewwriter.com

Orbis

17 Greenhow Avenue, West Kirby, Wirral, CH48 5EL
You can read about this magazine at www.poetrymagazines.org.uk. You can also search 'Orbis' on Facebook to view their page.

Poetry London

81 Lambeth Walk, London, SE11 6DX
www.poetrylondon.co.uk

Poetry Nation Review

4th Floor, Alliance House, 30 Cross Street, Manchester, M2 7AQ
www.pnreview.co.uk

Poetry Review

www.poetrysoc.com
Click on the 'poetry review' tab.

Poetry Scotland

91-93 Main Street, Callander, FK17 8BQ
www.poetryscotland.co.uk

Poetry Wales

57 Nolton Street, Bridgend, CF31 3AE
www.poetrywales.co.uk

Sentinel Literary Quarterly

Unit 136, 113-115 George Lane, London, E18 1AB
www.sentinelpoetry.org.uk

South Poetry Magazine

PO Box 3744, Cookham, Maidenhead, SL6 9UY

www.southpoetry.org

Staple Magazine

114-116 St Stephen's Road, Sneinton, Nottingham, NG2 4JS
www.staplemagazine.co.uk

The Wolf Magazine

3, Holly Mansions, Fortune Green Road, West Hampstead, London, NW6 1UB
www.wolfmagazine.co.uk

Online magazines and journals

Dragon Heart Press

www.dragonheartpress.com
Dragon Heart is a digital publisher of poetry in the UK. Submissions welcomed – details online. Details of competitions on website.

Free Verse: A Journal of Contemporary Poetry and Poetics

http://english.chass.ncsu.edu/freeverse
Bi-annual electronic journal publishing free verse. Publishes US work but also invites English language submissions from outside America. Submission information on the website.

Glasgow Review

www.glasgowreview.co.uk
Publishes poetry, art, articles, short stories. Submission information online.

Osprey Journal

www.ospreyjournal.co.uk
Scotland's international journal of literature, arts and ideas. This online journal publishes poetry, short stories, art, reviews and articles.

Pens on Fire

www.pensonfire.com

Online magazine for short fiction and poetry. Guidelines for submission on the website. Helps give many writers their first by-line.

Poetry Monthly

www.poetrymonthly.com
Published 1st of each month. Publishes contemporary poetry. The magazine is a free pdf file. Submissions information on the website.

For a comprehensive list of poetry magazines, online emagazines and journals (as well as poetry competitions and festivals), visit www.poetrylibrary.org.uk. You will also find extensive lists of magazines in the Writers' and Artists' Yearbook: www.writersandartists.co.uk.

Performance venues for poets

Apple and Snakes

www.applesandsnakes.org

The Poetry Café

poetrycafe@poetrysoc.com
Visit www.poetrysoc.com for further details.

The Poetry Library

www.poetrylibrary.org.uk

Scottish Poetry Library

www.spl.org.uk

Book List

Blazing Fruit: Selected Poems 1967 – 1987
By Roger McGough, Penguin Poets, London, 1990.

Book Proposals – The Essential Guide
By Stella Whitelaw, Need2Know, Peterborough, 2011.

Collected Poems
By Norman MacCaig, Chatto & Windus, London, 1993.

Collected Poems
By Edwin Muir, Faber & Faber, London, 2008.

Collected Poems
By Sylvia Plath, Faber & Faber, London, 2002.

The Collected Poems of Robert Burns
By Robert Burns, Wordsworth Editions, Herefordshire, 1994.

Collected Poems of Ted Hudges
By Paul Keegan (ed), Faber & Faber, London, 2005.

Creating Fictional Characters – The Essential Guide
By Jean Saunders, Need2Know, Peterborough, 2011.

The English Poems of John Milton
By John Milton, Wordsworth Editions, Herefordshire, 1994.

Lupercal
By Ted Hughes, Faber & Faber, London, 1985.

Nine Modern Poets: An Anthology
By E.L. Black (ed), Macmillan Education Ltd, Oxford, 1966.

Opened Ground: Poems 1966 – 1996
By Seamus Heaney, Faber & Faber, London, 2002.

The Penguin Book of First World War Poetry
By George Walter (ed), Penguin Classics, London, 2006.

The Prophet
By Kahlil Gibran, William Heinemann Ltd, US, 1972.

Publishing Poetry – The Essential Guide
By Kenneth Steven, Need2Know, Peterborough, 2010.

The Road Not Taken and Other Poems
By Robert Frost, Dover Publications, US, 1993.

Selected Poems 1946 – 1968
By R.S. Thomas, Bloodaxe Books, Newcastle upon Tyne, 1986.

Selected Poems: D.H. Lawrence
By James Fenton (ed), Penguin Poets, London, 2008.
Edited by James Fenton.

Selected Poems: Tennyson
By Christopher Ricks (ed), Penguin Classics, London, 2007.

The Waste Land and Other Poems
By T.S. Eliot, Faber & Faber, London, 2002.

Writing Dialogue – The Essential Guide
By Jean Saunders, Need2Know, Peterborough, 2011

Writing Non-Fiction Books – The Essential Guide
By Gordon Wells, Need2Know, Peterborough, 2010.

Writing Romantic Fiction – The Essential Guide
By Jean Saunders, Need2Know, Peterborough, 2011.

Talk, workshop or reading

If you would like to inquire about talks, workshops or readings – either for a school or writers' group – please contact Kenneth Steven via the email address below. Fees and future itineraries may then be obtained: info@kennethsteven. co.uk.